Rogue River Diaries

*The Collins family story of resilience,
kindness, strength,
and laughter*

Rod Collins

Bright Works Press

Rogue River Diaries

Bright Works Press
www.brightworkspress.com

© 2023 Rodney D. Collins
All rights reserved

Paperback ISBN: 978-0-9965394-5-6
Hardcover ISBN: 978-0-9965394-6-3

Cover photo: ©Epkes Creative/Adobe Images
Cover and interior design, editing, and production
   Eva Long • Long On Books
   www.longonbooks.com

Printed in the United States of America

*This is my story and the story of my family,
filtered through years of events and polished tales that
may only reflect events as I wish to remember them.
There are questions I now have for my parents and
grandparents that will go unanswered,
details lost in time because no one is now alive
to remember and relate those events.*

*I dedicate these stories
to my children and my grandchildren.
I only hope I can provide answers to questions that
may not occur until they, too, reach the edge of old age.*
~ Rod Collins, 2023

The Early Years

FOR WHATEVER REASON, AND MUCH to my childhood disgust, I was born a Californian, a fact I kept hidden from my Oregon friends for years.

I was born in Santa Monica, California on June 5, 1941, some six months before the Pearl Harbor attack by the Japanese. The exact reason my parents were in Santa Monica was never really clear to me. But a story told by my father, John Durant Collins, about laying a flagstone driveway and building a flagstone swimming pool for actor James Cagney, and comments by my mother, Wanda Mae Troop Collins about living in North Hollywood may explain the location.

My first clear memories are of life in Butte Falls, Oregon. In 1943 and 1944 my father worked as a log cutter for Medco (Medford Corporation). The Department of Defense listed certain occupations as critical to the war effort, and because lumber was considered a critical material, loggers weren't drafted at that time. Later in the war as manpower became scarce, loggers were subject to the draft. But that's later in the story.

We lived in what I remember as a nice single-story house with a backyard, a swing, and a clothesline. Mother cooked and canned on a wood cook stove. At age two-and-a-half, I had the run of the neighborhood and could go "visiting." It was, for the most part, a safer world for children and would remain so in rural Oregon until I was in my teens.

For me at least, it was a happy time. I remember my mother playing the guitar and singing "You Are My Sunshine." I remember community dances and watching Mother dance the night away. As I reflect, it's something of a jolt to think she was just barely 21 years old.

She and Dad often took pity on lonesome soldiers and invited them to the house for a home cooked meal. Often as not, the meat was fresh venison killed by Dad or one of the neighbors. Beef was in short supply to the civilian population as demand rose to feed the hundreds of thousands of military men, so we made do with fresh fish and illegal venison.

A story I've heard repeated in various forms over the years was about a man cutting firewood and hauling it home in his wagon. Hidden under the wood was a freshly killed deer. The local game warden stopped him and chatted for a few nervous minutes, and then said, "Well, I guess you better get your wood home before it bleeds to death."

I don't remember any other children in Butte Falls. But there were plenty of adults, including soldiers who were being trained by the U.S. Army in Camp White. Camp White was located on the current site of White City, a few miles north of Medford, Oregon on Highway 62. The Veterans Administration Domiciliary still operates a residential facility there for veterans.

Later, I listened to Dad talk about what a mean son-of-a-bitch the camp commandant was, ordering forced marches to Butte Falls with full field packs, a distance of about twenty-six miles, followed by night maneuvers. My Dad's dislike grew stronger when some soldiers were killed by an accidental explosion up in the country east of Butte Falls. I clearly remember hearing the "boom" and asking Mother what the noise was.

Timber falling was done with hand tools: double-bitted axes, falling saws and bucking saws, hardwood wedges, and mauls to drive the wedges into the cut, and the ever-present kerosene bottle, usually a quart bottle of some kind with a cork stopper and a loop of twine or old boot lace for a handle. Loggers sprinkled kerosene on the saw blade to keep the tree pitch from binding the saw to the cut. Buckers used an iron bar with tongs driven into the underside of logs for support when under-bucking was necessary. My memories and the few pictures from the old logging days include the red Effanem crusher, a felt hat worn by most loggers. Along with staggered britches, it was a proud badge that marked them as loggers.

It was hard work done by iron-hard men. There were no fat loggers, or at least no live ones. My dad stood a half-inch short of six-foot, had broad shoulders and a thick chest, but he only weighed 145 pounds when he was "broke in" to the log cutting.

Sometimes on really big trees log cutters would use springboards to get above swell-butted trees. I have a print of a Ken Brauner painting that depicts two timber fallers using springboards and a long, limber falling saw working on a big fir tree that must have been six feet in diameter. In the painting, the fallers have undercut the tree which was done in real life by first making a horizontal cut in the trunk with the saw, and then chopping downward at about a 30-degree angle to make a big triangle-shaped undercut. On big trees, it took quite a while just to make the undercut.

I remember Dad coming home smelling of fresh sawdust and kerosene. He'd take off his calked boots we called "cork" boots on the back porch and slip on a pair of leather slippers. For my children and grandchildren who don't remember, cork boots had short metal spikes built into the soles. Corks gave the logger traction on slippery wood. I'm not sure cork boots are worn anymore. At least I don't know of any loggers who use them. I suppose Vibram boot soles have replaced calks.

Ken Brauner's is pretty accurate, but my photo of the painting is just a little "off."

But I digress I think, unless the paraphernalia of our lives is interesting to my intended readers. I know they were important to us at the time. It was part of earning a living for our family. Dad spent a part of the weekend cleaning and then oiling his boots with Neatsfoot oil to keep them waterproof. And when an axe handle wore out, he spent several patient hours shaping a hardwood handle to fit the axe head. He'd break a bottle and pick through the shards until he found one the right shape and then use the sharp glass to carefully shave the head of the handle down. When the axe head fit to his satisfaction, he would drive the handle into the axe head, trim the end above the axe head with a hacksaw, and then drive small metal wedges into the top of the handle to swell the wood and fix the handle in place. He sharpened the axe head with a round whetstone until he could shave hair with it, and then finished the job by soaking the newly seated axe handle in a bucket of water overnight to swell the wood.

I still use this method for seating an axe handle. And I still have a couple of round axe stones. I'm just not as careful about my axes as Dad was because I don't have to make a living with one.

Dad also wore black Can't Bust 'Em jeans with the bottom hems of the pant legs cut off. The purpose of "staggering" the pant legs like this was to make sure the material would tear if the logger got hung up on a stob and had to run to keep from getting clobbered by a falling limb or a tree. I really don't know if it helped. It might have been more a matter of tradition than a matter of safety. (A note about stobs: a stob was any short limb sticking out of a log. When big trees were cut down, the process of falling would generally break limbs off the tree, leaving short, sharp "stobs" along the trunk.)

There is a story about a logger who slipped off a log and ran a stob through his britches and a few inches up under his tailbone. His feet couldn't touch the ground, so he couldn't push himself up and off the stob. He was hollering for his partner who came running and jumped up on the log which in this story was slender and flexible. Every time his partner took a step it bounced the log and the guy would holler in rhythm to the steps, "Don't, don't, don't run." Dad once told me loggers had been killed in a thousand different ways, and a different thousand waited for the unwary.

And one more thing: all the loggers I remember wore red suspenders called galluses that held up their Can't Bust 'Em's. Gloves were white cotton with a red ribbed cuff. They didn't stay white very long.

But more about logging later. More important to the story was the black bear cub Dad poured out of a burlap sack one late afternoon. He told me later in life about how he and his log-cutting partner, Art Polk, fell a big, hollow snag. When it was on the ground, they heard a lot of growling and whining that had to be a bear and her cubs. They located the hole the mama bear used to get her cubs into the hollow of the tree.

Art wanted those cubs, so he stood on the log with his double-bitted axe raised to whack the mama bear if she put up a fight. Dad beat on the log, from the opposite side of the hole, of course. Dad said the old mama bear just oozed out of the hole and was gone before Art could react. While Dad kept watch to make sure the mama bear didn't decide to come back and make a fuss, Art took two cubs from the nest. And that's how I came to have a black bear cub for a pet. Mama rigged up a nursing bottle and we hand fed it. But it grew rapidly and was soon bigger than I was. It would climb up on my back and wrap its strong arms around my neck. When that happened, I couldn't get loose, and I would holler for Mom.

Mom, Me and "the Bear"

We kept the bear for a few months, but as it grew it had to be chained to keep it from hurting anyone. I don't think the cub ever had a name. Dad finally gave it to a man who ran a service station on the highway in Talent, Oregon, a town on the old Highway 99 between Ashland and Medford. The man with the service station kept it in a cage as a tourist attraction until it got too big and too mean to be safe around people.

When I asked Dad what happened to "my" bear, he told me they had taken it up in the Ashland watershed and turned it loose. On one of our fall hunting trips years later, he confessed the bear had been shot because it had become too mean and too angry with people to run free. Dad also said it was a mistake to try and tame wild animals, and cruel to boot. He wasn't one to look back much once something was done, but he said he regretted taking those cubs from their mama.

Other Memories from Butte Falls

- Riding on my Uncle Darrel's shoulders while he tried to find the trail to the falls in Butte Creek in the canyon below town. I remember being disappointed when we couldn't find the trail down to the creek because I "knew" the way to the falls. Didn't.

- Being stung on the neck by yellow jackets while following the men down a brushy trail to fish the creek in below Fish Lake. My Dad put me on his shoulders and carried me out.

- Losing my blue dress hat in Fish Lake. My memory says we were in a rowboat, the wind blew my hat off and it sank before we could retrieve it. During one of those "Remember When" times with my mother, I told her about losing my hat in Fish Lake. She insisted there never was a hat, yet there it is in the next photo. I guess she forgot.

- Riding in an army jeep, one of those little ¼ ton 4x4 vehicles that some say won WWII for the Allies. I was impressed. Mom and Dad befriended some soldiers, fed them some venison and apple pie I guess, and they in turn invited us to visit their camp someplace up Butte Creek.

- Catching my first trout in the hole below the old Cobleigh Covered Bridge. I have a picture of that six-inch trout to this day. I think this ruined my life because I can't go too long without wanting to go fishing.

Mom, Dad, and me with 36 Ford and Travel Trailer at the California/Nevada State Line. Dad is 24, Mom is 20, and I'm a year old.

Monster Cobleigh Bridge trout, Butte Creek, below Butte Falls, OR

Tiller Mill

In the summer of 1944, we moved from Butte Falls, Oregon, to a lumber mill camp on the Tiller Trail Divide. The mill was located on the watershed divide between Trail Creek which flows roughly SE into the Rogue River at the little town of Trail, and Elk Creek which flows roughly NW and joins the South Umpqua River at the little town of Tiller, Oregon.

I remember the move clearly because I stepped in two pumpkin pies my mother set in the front seat of our 1936 Ford. I don't remember Mother giving me many spankings, but that time I got a good swat on my butt. I don't begrudge that one. There was one later I still resent.

Mom and Dad stuffed a utility trailer with household goods, packed the rest into the back seat and off we went…minus the two pumpkin pies. I'd like to tell you I stepped in the pies by accident, but even my polished memory can't quite shake the notion that I might have done it on purpose.

Our house in Tiller Mill was built out of rough-cut lumber, but it had a small, covered front porch, and three rooms. The first room was the kitchen which had the usual counters, a sink with a graywater drain, open cupboards, a wood cook stove, and a table and chairs.

The next room was a living room complete with wood stove for heat. I don't remember much else about the living room except a nice area rug on the floor, and Dad's rifles and his fishing poles hanging on the wall between the living room and the kitchen. I remember Mother once saying the carpet was new at the time. (My impression from her stories in later life was one of a happy young couple coming out of the Great Depression years and getting their household goods together for the first time.)

What I remember about the bedroom, other than the bed, was all of Mother's canning on the floor under the bed. My shifty memory says there wasn't much room left under there.

I think my mother's prudence was prompted by some hard times in the first years of their marriage. Dad once told me a story about when they lived in Hawthorne, Nevada sometime in 1940. The work was shut down for a couple of months and he and Mom were down to $5 and a tank of gas for his '32 Ford. They were eating cornmeal mush without sugar or milk and trying to figure out what to do next when a man offered Dad a job laying pummy blocks for a store the man was building. Dad said he knew how to do the work, but he hadn't been eating too well and wasn't sure if he could stand up to the work. The man sent him to a restaurant and told him to order a steak dinner to get his strength back. That got them started again.

A song from those times sums it all up pretty well: "Brother Can You Spare a Dime?" I found a book in my dad's possessions after he died. The title was the same: *Brother Can You Spare Me A Dime?* On the inside cover, in Dad's handwriting, is the inscription, "Property of John Collins. Please return." That he valued the book speaks volumes to me.

I think the Great Depression marked Mom and Dad's generation, the children of the Depression, to a depth that was unshakable. The memories of that time shaped their survival attitude. The very institutions they relied on had failed, from the stock market to the banks. Life savings were wiped out when banks closed, land was repossessed, unemployment was staggering because there were few jobs but many workers, and there were no social safety nets like welfare or unemployment insurance at that time. In Dad's terminology, it was "root hog or die." They had to rely on themselves.

At his death in 2000, Dad left Mother a new Dodge diesel pickup, a good Buick car, a pickup camper, a 14-foot fishing boat, a brick house on irrigated acreage they had owned for over forty years, and $100,000 cash. He left her debt-free.

But back to Tiller Mill. In the year of 1943-44, there was no electricity closer than the town of Trail some 10 miles back down the dirt and gravel road that served as highway. We relied on coal oil lamps. Plumbing was absent. We carried buckets of drinking water from a wooden flume across the road that carried spring water down from the hills and into a pond; we heated water on the wood cook stove for washing dishes, clothes, and bodies; and we used an outhouse for sanitation. Bathing took place in a big, galvanized tub.

I should note the steam engines that powered the mill also provided hot water for showers. Thursday night was women's night at the shower house. Saturday was men's night.

An Aladdin lamp was the Cadillac of coal oil lamps. It operated with a glowing "mantle" a lot like the old Coleman gas lanterns, and it produced 60 watts of light.

You were living the good life with an Aladdin lamp. So, we didn't live in the dark…exactly. (I still own an Aladdin in good operating condition just in case the power goes out.)

The House Fire

EARLIER THAT MORNING, I HAD gone across the road, which in itself was a big no-no, and gotten wet by wading in the pool below the flume, another no-no, and compounded my sins by standing under the stream pouring from the overhead flume. To say Mother was irritated would be mild in comparison to her mood when she caught me. I'm pretty sure I got swatted on my butt.

At any rate, she put me in the backseat of our car and drove the short distance to the cookhouse where families could shop for basic foods, things like bacon, canned milk, flour, and beans. I was much too young to remember anything else folks could buy, but I do remember John Taylor, the mill cook. The Taylor family remained friends with Mom and Dad after the milll closed. Taylor managed the Flounce Rock Ranch up river from Shady Cove for quite a few years. He boarded my horse Shorty, but again that's later in the story.

When we came back out of the cookhouse, someone yelled, "Your house is on fire," and pointed to the small logged-off canyon that separated our place from the other houses in the camp. I remember a column of black smoke, probably from the tar paper the mill owners used for roofing.

By the time we drove back to the house, it was pretty much gone. Everything my parents owned was destroyed: clothes, dishes, hunting rifles, fishing poles, canned goods, and Mother's money stash. The only item rescued was a pressure cooker that was on the floor under the kitchen table.

A Forest Service employee, Bud Lowell, was already at the house when we drove up. He asked Mother where Dad kept his rifles. Mom told him on the wall between the kitchen and the living room. Bud said he'd get them, but when he started crawling into the house another man grabbed him by the ankles and pulled him back out the door. Bud managed to grab hold of Mother's pressure cooker which was sitting under the kitchen table. It was the only thing saved from the fire.

Later in life, Mom told me she had thought seriously about leaving me home while she drove over to the cook house. In retrospect, she said, she was glad she hadn't, and I have to admit I am too.

When Dad got back out of the woods that afternoon, the only clothes he owned were the ones he had on. We spent the next few days living in Mom and Dad's 16-foot travel trailer before moving into another house up by the mill pond.

The loggers and the mill workers all pitched in and raised about $300 to get us going again. That was the second time my mom and dad had to start over. They would have to do this two more times.

Our second Mill House in Tiller Mill

As I reckon it, they started over once during the Great depression when Dad lost the five dump trucks he owned because the work on the All-American Canal, being built to carry water from the Colorado River to Los Angeles, was halted for several months. They started over again after the house fire. They started over again when Dad came back from his tour in the Army, which I'll get to later in the story. And they started over when Dad was misdiagnosed with a heart attack in 1956.

But back to the house fire. We moved into another mill house, one right across the road from the mill pond. I could stand on the front porch and watch my dad bring turns of logs with a "Cat" and an arch right down the road in front of the house. The road was both skid trail and mill road. It was dusty as all get out in the summer and a sea of mud in the winter.

Dad was "skinning" cat at that time. He operated a big, tracked Caterpillar called a "Cat" pulling an arch. The arch was hooked to the Cat, the bull line on the winch behind the Cat ran through a pulley on top of the arch, and several logs would be hooked by chokers to the bull line. The term for the men that set the chokers was the unimaginative "choker setter."

Think of a choker as flexible braided metal cable that had a metal nub on the end (the nubbin'). The nubbin end of the cable was pushed or pulled around the end of a log, and then the nub pushed into the slot of a metal piece (the bell) that slid up and down on the cable. The other end had a braided loop that was "hooked" to the bull line of the cat. When the bull line was pulled tight, the loop around the log was pulled tight. The cat skinner winched the logs up to the arch and lifted the front of the logs off the ground. The arch wasn't powered, but it had a set of tracks mounted on rollers. By getting the front of the logs off the ground, the Cat could pull a lot more logs down the skid road at one time.

Granddaughter Miquela and I spotted this old arch in the Lowell City Park. For perspective, Miquela was about five feet tall at the time of the photo. I don't think the red paint is the original color, although Allis-Chalmers built logging equipment that was painted red.

I'd watch Dad pull a "turn of logs" across three big logs buried perpendicular to the road in front of the steam donkey. A man working as a "knot bumper" would unhook the chokers from the logs and the cat would pull the chokers free. Then the donkey puncher would tighten two huge cables anchored to a brow log on the lip of the mill pond, and the turn of logs would roll and slide into the mill pond. I loved to watch because the steam donkey had a jumpy clutch and sometimes the lines would snap tight and throw big logs halfway across the pond.

Once, a neighbor's busy little black and white mutt (I remember it being Art Polk's dog…but I could be wrong) jumped up on the logs just as the donkey puncher engaged the clutch and the big cables snapped tight, throwing several logs and one dog into the pond. I was sure the dog was dead, but up he came and clawed his way onto a log just before another big log slammed into it. He hopped from log to log and made it safely back to shore.

That was the summer I waded in the ditch between the house and skid-trail/street and cut my left foot on a broken beer bottle. Ruined my new rubber boots in the process. I'm not sure, but I suspect ditch wading was another taboo I broke. Anyway, my always resourceful Mother patched up my foot, and I still carry the scar.

One of the highlights of my day was Dad coming home from the woods, smelling of kerosene, wood pitch, and honest sweat. He'd let me unlace his boots and then he'd slip on a pair of leather slippers, another one of those logger things they all seemed to own.

Dad home from a day of working in the woods. Note the Effanem crusher, the metal lunch bucket, the staggered pants, our dog Rusty, and a chicken in the background. I have no idea whose chicken it was. The pipes tell me we had water and a kitchen sink in this house.

The Collins family story of resilience, kindness. strength, and laughter

In the fall, before the rain and snow shut the logging down, my Aunt Patty, Dad's sister, brought her daughter Claudia to live with us in the mill house. Her husband, Uncle Bill Walsh, was in the Air Force in England at the time.

I have no memory of why Aunt Patty chose to move in with us. Maybe it was just because she had grown up in Dorena, Oregon, east of Cottage Grove and wanted to come back to Oregon from Southern California. Or maybe it was just because she loved her brother and was a great friend of Mother's. As a side note: Aunt Patty arranged the first meeting between Mom and Dad. It worked out, I think, because they had been married 60 years when Dad died.

Aunt Patty (Collins) Walsh, Uncle Bill Walsh in his Air Force Uniform, Claudia and Patty's youngest brother, my Uncle Dean Collins

Dad loved her I'm sure, but Patty had one habit that rankled him. She wanted to be a writer, and after everyone had gone to bed, she would sit at the kitchen table and write in her notebook until the wee hours of the morning. The only heat in the small house was the wood cook stove. Each evening Dad would split kindling to start his early morning fire so Mom could cook his breakfast. On one of our hunting trips later in life, he laughed and told me that nearly every morning he would wind up going to the woodshed and splitting more kindling because Aunt Patty burned all the kindling to stay warm at night. He even tried cutting extra kindling, but that didn't work. She just burned all the wood again, and when the house finally cooled off, then she went to bed.

Claudia, a year younger than my four years, became my first childhood friend, and remained my good buddy until her sad death at almost age five. I had a hard time understanding what had happened, and I missed her. She was Grandma Opal's favorite, too. I've included a photo taken the winter Aunt Pat and Claudia lived with us in Tiller Mill…house number two.

Cousin Claudia Walsh, age 3, winter 1944-1945

The Collins family story of resilience, kindness. strength, and laughter

Mother told me later in life that Claudia had choked on a buckle from a bra strap. When Aunt Patty dug it out with her finger to keep Claudia from choking, she must have scratched the child's throat with a fingernail. That led to the infection which killed Claudia. They were living at the time behind the Pig Creek Café that Aunt Patty owned between Eagle Point and the junction to Butte Falls.

Dogs and friend, winter Tiller Mill

You can see in the picture that the mill owners essentially logged every stick of usable timber that could be reached by high lead cable, which was a heck of a lot of the canyon and upper basin near the mill. Note the spar pole in the background of the picture. The only reason the little trees weren't logged was because the saws weren't set up to mill small poles in those days. I don't know who the smaller person is here, Claudia maybe, but the big dog is Rusty, our hound. I'll have a story or two later in time about Rusty hunting deer for us.

As I write, memories come floating to the surface like old friends unexpectedly dropping by for a visit. The local school district paid Mother to drive three young school children from Tiller Mill to the Trail Creek grade school. I got to ride along, and my memory tells me one trip was made in the snow before the road was plowed. The road went south and uphill from Tiller Mill, past the Tiller Creek Guard Station on top of the Tiller-Trail divide, where Bud Lowell and his family lived, and then a couple miles south and down to Dead Horse Canyon. The road was narrow, crooked, and dangerous, and I was sure Mom was going to run us into the canyon. Over the years, more than one log or lumber truck was wrecked on the last sharp corner on the west end of Dead Horse Canyon. At any rate, Mother spent part of that school year taking those children (whose names I don't remember) back and forth to school. Safely. Mom was always a good driver.

I was mainly an outdoor child, barefoot in warm weather, shirtless when Mom allowed, and basically unafraid of anything. But my memory of climbing in the trunk of our Ford and pulling the lid shut, and of then being trapped in the dark until Mother rescued me may explain my slight touch of claustrophobia. I have never liked confined places since. Here's a summertime photo of that car with me on the outside of the trunk, and my hound, Rusty. You'll note the parking area had yet to be insulted by a layer of gravel.

Rusty and our Ford

The Collins family story of resilience, kindness. strength, and laughter

Suddenly, Dad was gone "off to war." My grandparents, Ida Mae Mitchell Troop and Charles Augustus Troop were living with my mother and me in an apartment in Ashland, Oregon, and some mysterious creature called a baby was about to join our family. As summers go, it was an okay time. Uncle Darrel was there in time for the August birth of my new sister Gloria Dawn, and in fact he chose my new sister's name.

The trauma of having a new sibling didn't scare me very much. As the oldest Collins grandchild, the first male descendant in the Collins line, and as my father's son, I ruled in supreme confidence that I was king of the brood.

I have various memories of our time in Ashland:

- Riding in the rumble seat of a convertible car.
- Some older girls taking me swimming in the Ashland swimming pool.
- Grandma getting her breast caught in the wringer on the washer... and Grandpa laughing, which put his life at risk.
- My baby sister coming home from the hospital.
- Throwing my grandma a magazine and smacking her between the eyes, an effort that broke her glasses. I didn't get in trouble that time because I did exactly what she said. "Throw me that magazine, Rodney." (What do you expect from a four-year-old-boy?)
- Feeding the ducks and geese in the Lithia Park Pond.
- Sipping a foul-tasting brew called Lithia water, the mineral heavy water that some folks drank for their health. You can still get Lithia water from the fountains just downhill from the park in Ashland. And it's still foul tasting.

Clearer memories are related to living with Grandma and Grandpa Troop in Brea, California. That was my first experience in dealing with any older kids, and I didn't do well.

For starters, Mom's sister, Aunt Juanita Troop Hazelton and my cousins Leah and Terry were also living with Grandma and Grandpa. Leah was my age, and Terry was a couple years older. I think he was in something they called kindergarten, heading for the first grade. And when his left foot was squashed by a car, he got all the attention. My feelings of isolation were also aggravated by all the attention Mother was giving the new baby, Gloria.

Rod, Terry and Leah on the front porch of Grandma and Grandpa Troop's Brea house. (The front porch seems to have been a favorite photo site.)

I vaguely remember hearing a description of Terry's accident that still chills my bones. The story says Terry stepped off the curb in front of a car. He was barefoot as children often were in that time. The driver slammed on his brakes which caused the tires to slide. Somehow one of the tires wound up on top of Terry's foot. I still shudder when I think about bare feet and sliding tires. But kidlike, Terry was soon as fast on crutches as the rest of us on two legs.

More memories of Brea:
- Making friends with George, a little boy with a deep voice and my second friend in this life.

George is the bigger kid.

The Collins family story of resilience, kindness. strength, and laughter

- Vacation Bible School where I learned to sing "Onward Christian Soldiers."
- Leah hitting me with a brass hose nozzle. I chased her around the house and up on the back porch. Grandma caught me about to throw the nozzle at Leah. I don't remember what punishment I got that time. But, like a lot of things in this life, the perpetrator got away, and the responder got caught.
- Riding around the block with George on our tricycles.
- Walking a couple of blocks to the city swimming pool, which in those days cost a dime.

Mother's handwriting on the back of this photo reads: Taken just as Rodney and Leah came home from Sunday school. He has his new clothes on.

Grandpa Charlie Troop feeding chickens in his side yard.

In Brea Grandpa planted a big garden each year, kept rabbits and chickens and a mean goose he had given to me…and which we left with him when we packed up and headed back to Oregon.

The War

AS A FAMILY, WE WERE fortunate. None of our men were killed or injured during the war. At one point in time, late in the war, all men of draft age in our family were in some branch of the service.

My Uncle Charles Hazelton, 1945, age 28
He was mighty proud of his curly, red locks, which is why
he wore his sailor cap as far back on his head as he dared.

The Collins family story of resilience, kindness. strength, and laughter

Uncle Charles was on a destroyer that fought in the South Pacific. The only comment I ever heard him make about the war was to the effect his ship shot down a Japanese Zero.

Uncle Darrel Troop was a meteorologist for the Air Force, stationed first in Fairbanks (where he bunked with actor Jack Kelly who later played Bart Maverick on the TV program "Maverick"), and then on out to Adak Island where the Air Force built an air base as a deterrent to Japanese invasion.

Uncle Cliff Troop was in the Air Force and stationed in England.

Uncle Bill Walsh was in the Air Force, also stationed in England. His comment, made to me when he was in his seventies was that we were right in bombing "those bastards" into oblivion, meaning the German Nazis.

Mom's cousin Bob Frost was in a construction battalion that fought across Europe from D-Day to the end of the war. His unit liberated one of the numerous concentration camps in Germany. The only war story I remember him telling was of hiding under his caterpillar while the German's strafed and bombed the area his unit occupied. His only other comment was about the concentration camp his unit liberated. (I don't remember the name of the camp.) He said battle-hardened soldiers cried and some threw up after entering the camp.

Bob Frost, c. 1940, before WWII started

My father was drafted late in the war. After boot camp at Fort Lewis in Washington state, his company rode the train to New York where they were put on troop transport ships headed for Europe.

On one of our hunting trips later in life Dad told me his troop transport was six days from LaHarve, France, when the Germans surrendered. He said even though alcohol was prohibited, the whole bunch, sailors and soldiers alike got drunk in celebration. (And then he told me how the soldiers smuggled booze onto the boat by taping flat pint whiskey bottles to their ankles and then pulling socks over the bottles.) He was in Germany for several months with the Army of Occupation. He said the job of his Construction Battalion was rebuilding roads and restoring the infrastructure of the country. (I'm including a picture...not a very clear one...of Dad and one of his army buddies standing on a pile of rubble which was commonplace in Germany at the end of the war.)

Sergeant John Collins (left) and a buddy standing on a pile of rubble in Germany, 1945

When it came time to be discharged, an officer insisted he put his chevrons on his sleeves. He complied by using LePage's glue.

One of the happiest days of my life was when my dad came home in August of 1946. I clearly remember riding in a car from Brea to the Los Angeles train depot. We watched khaki clad men streaming off the train, and then Mother, with Gloria in one arm and holding my hand, pulled me forward. There was my dad, and my world was complete again. And I got a spanking that first afternoon I still resent.

Mother insisted Dad glue his stripes on one last time.

Dad was tired after a long trip that included crossing the Atlantic by troop ship, followed by a train ride from New York City to Los Angeles. There were bunks on the ships, but no real place to sleep on the train. Those who knew him in later life will understand when I say that after greeting the Troop and Hazelton clan, and after seeing his baby daughter for the first time, he took a nap…on a couch in the living room.

My memory says I couldn't stand him being asleep and not paying attention to me so I woke him up. He sat up, grabbed me, and gave me a wallop on the butt. In retrospect, I suspect he was wound pretty tight and reacted without thinking.

I learned in later life Dad and Mom were about to start over again. First, the allotments from the government were months late getting to Mother. So, she sold their travel trailer to raise some money. Second, home on leave, Uncle

Cliff loaned Dad's mechanics tools out to a friend. The tools were stolen and Cliff didn't have the money or the time to replace them. Third, Uncle Darrel, home on leave, took some buddies out partying and rolled Mom and Dad's 1936 Ford. It was a total wreck and there was no insurance. Darrel was shortly shipped to Fairbanks and didn't have the money or time to replace the car.

When Dad came home from Germany, he had $600 in severance pay, no tools, no car, no hunting rifle or fishing pole, no travel trailer, and no civilian clothes. But he did have a new baby daughter.

Gloria's first birthday, August 18, 1946

Given the sidewalk and the tree in the background, I believe this picture is of Gloria on her first birthday. That would make it August 18, 1946. It looks like Dad is wearing his army boots, which tells me we hadn't started back to Oregon yet.

The Collins family story of resilience, kindness. strength, and laughter

Mom and Gloria early 1946

Shortly after this picture was taken, Dad bought an old rattletrap 1936 Ford, packed it with our few remaining possessions and headed for Oregon. Two things are notable: First, cars were hard to come by because auto production all but ceased during the War. He was lucky to find one at all. Second, metals used in auto engines were softer than today, so motors tended to wear out quickly.

In terms of our "new" car, it had no headliner and no door panels, and Dad had to add a quart of oil every 100 miles. But, in typical John Collins fashion, it had a good set of tires. Grandpa Charlie used his ration stamps to buy them.

I think I neglect my Grandparents, Charles, and Ida Mae Troop in the telling of this story, so I want to try and make up for that because they were the ones who held it all together until the uncles, cousins, fathers and husbands came home.

I have fond memories of Grandpa Troop joking around and teasing us. He would take a bite of something from a plate of food and say, "That's so good it'd make a tadpole sit up and slap a whale." And he would make us mind our manners. He threatened to "slap you to sleep and slap you for sleeping" for some infraction of the mores of the culture and times. I'm not sure where "jerk off a leg and beat you with it" came from, but I'm fairly sure it came from that time.

I remember Grandpa Troop liked Limburger Cheese. I did too, and I still do, but I don't remember Leah or Terry being especially fond of it. Grandpa would hold a jar of Limburger under a kid's nose and say, "That'd make a tad pole sit up and slap a whale."

I also remember Grandma Ida doing dishes and singing old country gospels. One ran something like, "Cheer up my brothers and live in the sunshine, we'll understand it all by and by." Another was, "In the sweet by and by, we shall meet on God's beautiful shore." (I was a bit miffed at Mother when the singer at Grandma's funeral sang those songs. Completely broke me down, and I still tear up writing about it.)

Here is one of the few Brea photos not taken on the front porch, circa 1946.

Ida Mae Mitchell Troop and Charles Augustus Troop, Brea, California 1946

The Collins family story of resilience, kindness. strength, and laughter

Note: Grandpa Troop was the only grandparent to ever spank me. I was pestering the girls, Leah and the two little girls from across the street. When I wouldn't stop after he told me to, he popped me on the butt. I stopped. I don't think it hurt me, but it did get my attention.

And later Grandpa bought me an ice cream cone at the drugstore a couple blocks up the street, so maybe I wasn't completely in the wrong after all. The girls were not very nice to me most of the time.

The last tale of being spanked by Grandpa Troop and then taken to the drugstore for ice cream, brought to the surface the memory of a fire a block or two from the house, not too far from the drugstore. I remember fire trucks and a car being on fire. Some poor soul was working under his car at night, using a candle for light. The gas tank had leaked and the fuel on the ground below the tank caught on fire, blew the tank out, burned the car, and killed the man.

I'm including some miscellaneous photos, because I don't know where else to slot them in, and because they might be important to the Troop side of the family.

Clifford, Ida and Darrel Troop. The boys were home on leave.

One final comment about living in Brea: On an earlier visit, before the war, I remember going to a high school football game and hearing the crowd chant, Troop, Troop, Troop" whenever Uncle Cliff carried the ball. He was a highly recruited college prospect, but the war interfered. He was drafted almost immediately after graduating from high school and never played football at the college level.

And finally, I'm including a picture of Michael Troop, Cliff's oldest son, partly because it's the only picture I can find of him in Mother's photos. I think I recognize the cap guns as a Roy Rogers pair, a lot like the ones Grandma and Grandpa Troop gave me for Christmas a few years later.

Michael Troop and cap guns. The black and white doesn't do justice to his red hair.

Shady Cove

THE NEXT ELEVEN YEARS WERE what I fondly refer to as my Shady Cove years. My copy of Lewis A. McArthur's "Oregon Geographic Names" says:

Shady Cove is on the Rogue River between two and three miles south of Trail. The Post office is on the Crater Lake Highway near the concrete bridge which carries the highway over the river, but the cove itself is upriver a few hundred yards and on the southeast side of the stream. The name is descriptive of a little nook on the riverbank, but is not particularly applicable to the locality of the post office and the highway bridge. Shady Cove post office was established in September 1939, with

The Collins family story of resilience, kindness. strength, and laughter

Mrs. Lillian F. Hukill, postmaster. The compiler has been informed that the name Shady Cove was applied to the place upstream from the post office some years before the office was established, by one J. Powell of Medford.

I had to laugh when I read that description of our town. Unless you know where Trail, Oregon is, it doesn't do much to help locate the town. Sort of reminds me of the time in a large grocery story when I asked a smart mouthed clerk where I could find the peanut butter. He said, "Next to the jam." It might be better to say Shady Cove is on the Rogue River about 22 miles north of Medford.

It was August when we moved into the Holcomb Place. The fruit in the little orchard right off the front porch was ripe and ready to pick. And the yellow jackets were swarming the windfall pears from the two big trees flanking the side gate into the backyard. One of those yellow jackets stung me on the roof of my mouth when I bit down on a pear the yellow jacket was sharing with me.

The Holcomb Place, as we always referred to it, was an old homestead about five miles up Longbranch Creek west/northwest of Shady Cove. Longbranch Road was surfaced with good, hard-packed shale, but the half mile road up to the house was steep and rutted. In places, you needed tall tires to keep from dragging bottom. And in the wet season, you might have to chain up to get there. I remember the road climbing the first steep hill and then topping out on an open bench that sported scrub oak, Manzanita brush, a few runty bull pine, and chaparral.

The road ran north a half mile or so parallel to a rim-rock canyon, then looped to the right over a culvert pipe, wandered through the scrub oak, the chaparral, and slick-barked, red-stemmed Manzanita, and finally made a big 180-degree swing past the barn and up to the house. I remember our hound Rusty chasing a buck out through the chaparral across the little canyon. Rusty was prone to chasing deer, and more than once chased a deer up to my Dad. I was with Uncle Dean once when Rusty chased a big doe right past us. Dean shot that one.

I can't remember how many acres went with the Holcomb Place, but there was the old house, a small orchard in the yard just off the front porch with apricot, cherry, and apples trees, two big pear trees bracketed the gate to the back door, and there was a big barn, a chicken coop, what I remember as a couple of rabbit hutches, a fruit cellar dug into the hillside, a woodshed attached to the side of the house, and a privy.

The old house, old even then, was a single-story, wood sided, unpainted two-bedroom house with kitchen, living room and a breakfast nook. The floor planks had shrunk to the point that in some places I could peek through the cracks in the floor and see the ground under the house.

The first night we were there, Dad shot a deer feeding in the orchard. He used a hand-held spotlight, one of those that operated off a big nine-volt battery, and a rifle he borrowed from his little brother, Dean. Dad just stepped out on the front porch, shined the light into the orchard, picked out a set of reflected eyes from a deer and shot it. My recollection is that he cleaned and skinned it and then hung it in the fruit cellar. In the first six months we lived up Longbranch Creek, Dad killed nine deer to help feed us. Almost all were killed under a spotlight.

When deer season came, he bought a deer tag, and then killed a nice four-point buck under the spotlight so he would have a set of tagged antlers to account for the venison in the meat locker in Shady Cove.

Later in life, on one of our Fall hunting trips, I accused Dad of failing to teach me how to fish or how to hunt when I was growing up. He looked puzzled until I added, "All I know how to do is spotlight deer and snag salmon." That got a laugh.

Dad was concerned about the rusty stove pipe that led from the wood heating stove and up through the attic, maybe because of the fire that burned our mill house, so one of the first things he did was install a terracotta chimney. For the uninitiated, terra cotta is a type of baked clay.

As I remember, he went into the attic through a ceiling hatch, pulled the big terracotta pipe up into the attic and somehow managed to block the hatch when the chimney was in place. Mom finally handed him a wood auger (think hand cranked drill) and a thin keyhole saw through the small gap between the ceiling and the chimney. Dad drilled four holes in a square pattern in the end gable of house, and then used the saw to cut his way out. Mom propped an old home-made wooden ladder against the side of the house for Dad's ignoble escape from the attic.

On one of our hunting trips years later, I mentioned this event to Dad, but he denied ever doing a dumb thing like that. I'm wondering if his forgetter

The Collins family story of resilience, kindness. strength, and laughter

wasn't working overtime. (Remember Mom's insistence that there never was a blue dress hat?)

We had to use a privy, but after Dad piped water down from a spring above the house, we at least had gravity fed running water in the kitchen and a graywater drain. And he built a shower in one corner of the kitchen that used hot water from the wood cook stove. I think the capacity of the "boiler" on the side of the stove was about two gallons. Mixed with cold water, the hot water lasted long enough for a decent shower. The next person in line had to wait thirty minutes for the water to reheat.

I found it interesting that the water actually circulated because of the difference in temperature between the small "pressure" tank and the water boiler in the stove. I guess that would count as one of my first science lessons.

I'm also remembering bare electric light bulbs in the kitchen and in the living room. I could be wrong about that. I guess that's one of those minor facts lost in time.

The Holcomb Place barn looking east from the front porch of the old house.
I have no idea who the people in the picture are,
and I know our Ford wasn't white.
The car might have belonged to Elbert and Betty Hefly.

There are no photos of the old house itself, but photos of the barn, the old root cellar and the porch give a hint of how it all looked. It was what I would term "raw" and pretty well run down. But the house sheltered us, the barn sheltered the heifer Grandpa Truman Collins had given me, and the pig pen proved totally incapable of holding the pig we raised. Somehow or another, the pig could climb the fence. We would get up in the morning to find the pig on the back porch. He liked to root our dog Rusty out of his warm bed and sleep there.

As I look back, what seemed perfectly normal was a subsistence style of living that would have been the envy of any modern-day hippy child.

In looking at the picture of the barn it occurs to me I don't recall any fields. There was some open ground but no farm fields.

During the first few days, Dad bought a set of hand tools and found a job bucking logs behind two timber fallers who were using a new tool called a chainsaw. It may have been an improvement over the old misery whips, but it still weighed in at about 100 pounds. The brands of power saws I remember were Diston and Titan. On one of our hunting trips later in life Dad said he had no trouble keeping up with the fallers because the two of them were only falling about 10,000 to 12,000 board feet of timber a day. And that was in good, big timber.

Note: A few years later, on a bet, Dad used a hand bucking saw to cut his way half through a 36-inch fir log in 90 seconds. He had to stop halfway through because, as he put it, he didn't have to wind to finish like he would have when he was "broke in." Still, halfway in 90 seconds was simply a fine example of what was possible with a well sharpened bucking saw.

By late summer, Elbert and Betty Hefley moved from someplace in Southern California to the Holcomb place. Elbert had never worked in the woods before, but after Dad trained him, ("broke him in" to use the vernacular of the loggers) Elbert "Dud" Hefley never worked anyplace else. Dad said he was a natural when it came to falling timber.

Rattlesnake

Sleeping arrangements in the old house put Elbert and Betty in the "south" bedroom off the living room, Mom and Dad and Gloria in the "north" bedroom and me on a pallet in the northwest corner of the living room not far from a pot-bellied wood-burning stove. The front door of the house faced east into the small orchard.

One warm summer afternoon, Mother put Gloria in her crib, told me to nap on my pallet and closed the door to her bedroom. After about age three I was never much interested in afternoon naps, but I did as Mother told me even if I couldn't sleep. The front door was open to catch a little breeze. There was no screen door.

I heard this quiet raspy sound and saw a rattlesnake heading across the room for my pallet. I did the only thing I could think of which was to jump to my feet and yell, "Mama…snake! Mama…snake!" Mom rushed out the door and the snake retreated to the southeast corner of the living room. He coiled and had his rattles buzzing. Mom picked me up and put me up on her bed, took a .22 caliber revolver from a holster hanging on a peg over the headboard and commenced blazing away at the snake. She actually nicked it once. I'm thinking she reloaded the revolver once and emptied it again. I do know the floor and wall in the southeast corner of the living room were both peppered with .22 caliber bullet holes.

I clearly remember mother closing the bedroom door and telling me to stay on the bed. I also remember looking at the door and deciding the gap between the floor and door was too big to keep an old snake out. So, I stood on the bed with a pillow raised to smash the snake and then watched and waited. The shooting had awakened Gloria, but she was just staring wide-eyed through the bars of her crib.

I heard a bang bang bang of something pounding the floor. The banging went on quite a while before it stopped. Finally, Mom opened the bedroom door to tell us it was okay now. She took me across the room and opened the door to Elbert and Betty's room. She let me peek in at it. Sure enough, the snake was dead. Mom had chased that poor old snake into Elbert and Betty's room with a long pole and then proceeded to turn the front half of the snake into paper thin snakeskin. I'm sure the snake was dead long before she stopped pounding.

She left the snake where it was until Dad and Elbert got home from the logging woods in the late afternoon. I'm not sure where Betty had gone, but the stark truth is we were living three miles from the nearest neighbor, we had no car that day and of course there were no phone lines up Longbranch Creek Road.

Gloria and me riding Bob Walkner's stinky old horse.

Years later around an evening campfire in hunting camp I asked Mom and Dad if our move to town had anything to do with the rattlesnake in the house. They insisted it had nothing to do with that. I'm not sure I believe them even to this day.

That first fall and winter back in Oregon was a happy time. Elbert and Dad both worked until the woods shut down. That meant they had sufficient money to see them through the winter. (This predates Unemployment Insurance by a couple of years.)

During the summer and the fall seasons, Mom and Betty put up a dozen gallon jars of grape juice squeezed from the grapes growing on the place, canned dozens of quarts of salmon, and put up about one-hundred-quart jars of fruit…pears, cherries, apricots, and applesauce, and made grape jelly, black berry jam, apricot jam and I don't remember what else. The fruit cellar was stuffed. What I remember was straw-packed shelves with a facing board to keep the jars and the straw from falling off.

The Collins family story of resilience, kindness. strength, and laughter

*Gloria and I playing in the yard.
Note the fruit cellar in the background.*

We had quite a bit of snow that winter…at least a foot deep. Dad and Dud (Elbert's nick name) took a sheet of plywood and a sheet of tin roofing and made a toboggan. I had one ride down off the hill with Elbert. We wound up sliding across the road below the house and into the shallow pool below the culvert. I don't remember another ride.

But I do remember trudging through the snow with Dad and Elbert up the hill behind the house to a big fir snag. They took a long pole and used it to widen the cracks in the bark on the old fir snag. Big thick slabs of bark came tumbling down to be chopped into six-foot lengths and tobogganed down to the woodshed. I think of fir bark as our form of coal. It burned steadily and gave us a nice bed of coals.

Elbert and Betty were big in this stage of my life. Betty wasn't too sure she liked little boys, but she tolerated me because Elbert liked me. And they both doted on Gloria. I found this photo in Mother's keepsake pictures. No story of the Holcomb Place would be complete without it.

Elbert Hefley and Gloria, 1946 (Elbert loved little kids.)

Other memories of life at the Holcomb place:
- Betty Hefley in a swimming suit out in the yard, dancing in the rain.
- Holding a spotlight while Elbert and Dad gigged (speared) bull frogs from a pond not too far from the house.
- The adults playing cards.
- Pumping the peddles on Mother's player piano (and pretending I was actually working the keys.)
- Uncle Darrel coming by on his way home from Alaska to Brea, California. He had duffel bags full of huge weather balloons, Eskimo mukluks, Eskimo mittens and I don't know what else, tokens of his stay in Fairbanks and on Adak Island.

Uncle Darrel's visit started a round of conversation about homesteading in Alaska. I remember how distressed I was because there wouldn't be any kids and there wouldn't be any schools to go to. Mother explained how we could get our lessons over the short-wave radio, but I remember thinking, "That won't work."

Ultimately, I believe what a move to Alaska would mean in physical distance between Mom and the Troop clan finally settled the issue. And I remember being glad. Now, in this late stage of life, I have to wonder what my life would have been like if we had homesteaded in Alaska's Matanuska Valley. I'd probably wound-up farming cabbages.

At any rate, our subsistence lifestyle came to an end in the spring of 1947. Dad bought a small city lot and two one-room shacks in the unincorporated town of Shade Cove. We'd probably call them cabins now. Think big wooden tents. The shacks were an identical 16' by 20'. Elbert and Betty lived for a time in one and we crowded into the other. We still used an outhouse, and we went back to carrying water for the house...this time from a water spigot in the yard of the little two-man planning mill across the unsurfaced road that played the role of street back then.

Cousin Dwight Collins, Gloria and I perched on the trunk of the old 1936 Ford Dad and Mom bought right after the war.
This picture was probably taken in the summer of 1947.

"Raw" followed us down off the hill. There was an awful lot of dirt to contend with. I can't remember a single lawn at any house in Shady Cove at that time.

Old Rusty had an extreme hatred of porcupines. He would just bore in and kill them. And then he might be gone for a couple of day before heading home with a mouthful of quills. Dad finally decided the Holcomb Place wasn't good for the hound, so Rusty went to live with Uncle Dean on the Reese Creek farm.

We replaced Rusty with twin black hounds and called them Mack and Mickey. Mickey was sweet tempered, but Mack was a nasty brute and damned near killed Mickey in a fight. Dad got rid of Mack. Don't know how, but I have suspicions.

Mickey was run over crossing the bridge between the Summer House and town. I saw him but couldn't bring myself to admit it. But when I got home, I cried and told Mom that Mickey was dead. Grandpa Troop went and got him, and we buried him behind the house. I think that was my first cowardly act.

Grandpa Troop retired from Shell oil along about this time, sold the Brea House, bought a new Chevy pickup and a travel trailer. He and Grandma Ida showed up in the late fall of that year and stayed quite a while. I have a picture someplace of that trailer and the snow that fell that winter. I'll see if I can scrounge it up and add it here. Sometime later, and I can't remember exactly when, they bought a small house in Talent, Oregon.

Grandpa Troop and his trailer behind the shacks.

That winter, it got so cold in the trailer that Grandpa's false teeth froze in a glass of water he put on the floor by his bed. He brought the glass into the house to thaw his teeth out. When Mother saw it she started laughing. He did too. In retrospect it seemed like they were both just full of fun. As sister Debbie says, Mom's fun meter was always set on high. I think the same can be said of Charlie Troop.

Beetle Bugging

BEETLE BUGGING WAS THE FINE art of dragging a beetle bugging hook in a series of hard horizontal jerks across the bottom of a big sandy hole in the Rogue River. The object was to snag the salmon that kegged up for the night. And, no, it wasn't legal even then. Dad said if the Game Commission had outlawed a way to hunt or fish, it was because it worked. In defense of our law breaking, there just weren't a lot of us living in the Rogue Valley in those days, so we didn't damage the fish runs very much. Our best night was 12 salmon…all of which were canned and then eaten the next winter. I really miss all of that.

To make a beetle bugging hook, take a large treble hook, say three inches long, slip a piece of copper tubing long enough run from the curves on the hooks to just under the eye; plug the bottom of the tube with a cloth; pour melted lead in the tube and let cool; clean away the spatters; put it away because the only place you can legally fish with one is in the ocean. There you have it.

A salmon Dad most likely snagged out of the Rogue River. We were living in the Holcomb place at the time.

Rogue River, C. 1939, Grandpa Troop in the center, Uncle Darrel on the left, and an unknown on the right.

But back to life in Shady Cove. The school yard was half a block down the street from the shacks. All spring I hung on the fence and watched kids playing in the school yard during recess. For some reason I can't remember and probably didn't understand even then, I wasn't allowed on the playground during school hours.

The schoolhouse was a two-room affair with a folding divider separating the two rooms, a stage on the south end of one room, a cloak room, and a little office for the principal. There was no gymnasium, no indoor plumbing. You did your business in a big outhouse, but there was one for the girls and one for the boys, so some modesty was maintained. Hand washing was done at an outside water spigot.

These crude facilities were gone by the time I was in second grade, replaced by a new wing on the old building, complete with restrooms, a cafeteria, library and classrooms. I think it was during my fourth year at Shady Cove Grade School a gym was built. And it wasn't much…jut a big barn of a building with a concrete floor, and unfinished on the inside. But we did have baskets for basketball and a stage and dressing rooms for sports.

Dad owned the Shell service station at that time. He and other local businessmen, including Ben Nork senior, got together with the school board and pushed to build a gym. I do not know where the money came from.

The Collins family story of resilience, kindness. strength, and laughter

*The Shell Station in Shady Cove, 1949.
Dad is second from the left.*

The ball field was a big dirt lot, maybe two acres in size. Ben Nork senior used to bring his grader to the field and blade it smooth. His son Benny and I would pick rock.

An enterprising soul put together a laundromat, sort of, in an unfinished shed on the south end of town on the first street beyond Indian Creek. It was just open studs with a roof. To my knowledge it was never sided, just framed up and roofed. For a quarter, you could wash a tub of clothes in a new-fangled electric machine. As I recall, there were two such machines… and I don't remember a dryer.

But I do remember meeting a little boy there at the laundromat who was later to become my lifelong friend. I'd like to say we were instant best friends, but that wouldn't be true. Benny Nork, junior and I were instant enemies.

I'm not sure why he was hanging out at the laundromat, but I know his family lived in a low roofed red painted log house, with white stripes marking the calking. It looked pretty then, and it remains so in my memory today. The only flaw was the light that slipped through the few broken chinks in the caulking, but that was only obvious at night. And maybe it only looked pretty to me because painted houses were the exception then.

Somehow, thinking of the two-machine laundromat let an old memory leak through the Mother Curtain of time. I think my mother was always trying to sissy me up, because I had a stuffed doll, a Raggedy Andy. I lost it at the laundromat…either there or someplace else in the going to or coming from.

I must have depended on it for comfort. Otherwise, I wouldn't remember losing it. We remember most those things that were important at the time.

The only thing I remember from that long summer was picking wildflowers for Mom, rolling a big agate boulder to the shack from a dry wash about quarter mile from the house, and fishing Hyatt Lake with my dad, my Grandpa Troop, and Uncle Darrel. We camped at Little Hyatt Lake that time. Grandpa made hotcakes in a cast iron skillet heated over a wood fire. He'd flip the skillet to turn the hotcakes over. They almost always landed raw side down…almost. I remember laughing when he misjudged his hot cake flipping and one split down the middle on the edge of the skillet. He laughed, too. He was like that. I think I learned to chuckle about most things from him.

First Days of School

THE SUMMER ENDED, AS ALL summers do, and I was no longer forbidden to use the playground because now I was a big kid. I was in school. My memories of the first day of school are pretty sharp and clear. Mrs. Bell was our first teacher, replaced later in the year by Mrs. Johnson, a teacher I liked better than Mrs. Bell.

The classroom for first and second graders was on the stage, and it was a bit crowded. Mrs. Bell gave us a few crayons and a picture of a robin. Kenny Williams, a little kid about my size, dressed in a new black t-shirt with red and white stripes, colored his robin blue, for which he was publicly scolded by Mrs. Bell. First, he hadn't waited until he had permission to start coloring the picture. "Second," she said, "robins are red, not blue."

In retrospect, I don't think school ever improved for Kenny after that. It was a downer from day one and pretty much stayed that way for him. Kenny died in his mid-fifties, so I never had a chance to talk to him after I started writing this tale of remembrance.

On the plus side, Mrs. Bell asked if any of us knew how to write any words. Marion Flowers said she could. She wrote "the" on the blackboard. I was miffed because I didn't know that word, and being miffed started my pursuit of knowing stuff, so that by second grade I was reading western novels. I reckon I caught up with that smart girl by then. You know how it is; once you break the code, reading is just a matter of adding to your vocabulary.

The Collins family story of resilience, kindness. strength, and laughter

The summer between my first and second grade was marked by a temporary move with Bob and Marciel Frost into a ramshackle, unpainted, two-story farmhouse just a few miles north of Grants Pass. Bob and Dad drove cats and Tournapulls as the Sexton Mountain Pass section of the new highway was being built between Grants Pass and Canyonville. The story goes that during the War an army convoy spent nearly twenty-four hours traveling from Canyonville to Grants Pass, a distance of about sixty miles. The military never forgets, so that was the first stretch to be built for what eventually became I-5. Military convoys might need to move a lot faster than the old highway permitted. I think our military people were also impressed by the German Autobahn system of highways. I know General Eisenhower pushed for the interstate system after he was elected President.

That was a long summer for me. Only one kid about my age lived close by, and when he peed on me, I hit him in the nose. His nose bled and there went my one and only playmate. Mother and Marciel tried hard to keep me entertained with crawdad fishing…using a willow pole, a piece of bacon tied on piece of string…and swimming in the Rogue River. They even set up a store and stocked it with canned goods. They would come and buy stuff from me. But I wasn't fooled, and it was a pretty dull business for me.

I had yet to learn how to swim. So later that year, at the Trail Creek swimming hole, Uncle Bill Walsh taught me to swim in about three minutes. Convinced me I could float. So, I did, and then started dog paddling.

The Summer House

WE LIVED IN THE SHACK for most of two years before moving into the summer house. The summer house is still there, but the big screen porch that ran along the river side of the house and around the west end has been enclosed and added to the living space of the house. If you turn east onto the road to the Cove just before the south end of the Shady Cove bridge, the first driveway on the right travels uphill a bit and marks the old summer house. The trees have grown enough to make it hard to see these days.

In 1949, I turned eight and enjoyed the summer of a lifetime. My cousin Terry, bigger and older than I was by about four years, came and stayed the whole summer. We could both swim by then, so every morning took us down a trail from the house, across the gravel road, and to the sandy beach at the swimming hole in above the bridge. I can't say for sure if Terry could stand that cold water better than I could, but about ten minutes of swimming saw me shivering and sitting on the sand in the sun.

The flood of 1964 took out the bridge and all the sand on the beach of the swimming hole. With the river now tamed by the Lost Creek Dam, I reckon the sandy beach will just stay in my memory, but never in reality.

Mom had one rule: Do Not Swim Across the River. Now kids are as good as jailhouse lawyers when it comes to rules, so Terry and I would only swim half-way across, and then turn around. I'm sure if Mom ever caught us, we would have been grounded and denied swimming privileges for the summer. That said, when I got in trouble, the punishment consisted of "no swimming today." That threat was enough to keep me in line. Most of the time.

A Note About Veterans

MOST SOLDIERS CAME BACK FROM the war addicted to nicotine. Heroes all of them. GI Joe. Short haircuts. A model for the young boys of America. So Terry and I stole two cigarettes and we smoked them in the hut we had built. As luck and cigarette smoke would have it, Mom caught us.

She laid out eight cigarettes on the kitchen table, four for each of us. And we smoked them. Terry threw up, sicker than a dog. I smoked mine… and liked them. I did not get sick. But I did not become a true smoker until my freshman year in college. I blame the vets I knew for getting me hooked. The vets I attended college with were irascible. They sat in the back of the classrooms and smoked. So I did, too.

Back To Summer

COUSIN MIKE TROOP, UNCLE CLIFF's son, joined Terry and me in our river escapades for almost a month. Grandpa Troop had a new Chevy pick up and hauled us around quite a bit, sometimes to the warmer water of the Trail Creek swimming hole, sometimes to the warmer water of Elk Creek so we could swim without freezing our buns off.

We always rode in the bed of the pickup with our backs against the cab, which was fine, except Grandpa chewed tobacco, and he spit out the window as we traveled. The slipstream carried a fine mist of tobacco juice around the cab and into the bed of the pickup. Terry and Mike, being a heck of a lot bigger than I was made sure I rode on that side of the pickup.

Visitors, And Then Some:

I SUPPOSE IT ISN'T KIND of me to think like this, but a lot of our Oklahoma relatives showed up that summer, generally empty handed. Dad had partnered up with Clay Knotts to buy the Shell station in town, made possible by a loan from Grandpa Troop. I guess the word got out that we were "rich" and living in a big house on the river. The upshot was we saw a lot of relatives that summer, some for the first time, and some for the last time.

Mom told me later in life we had company every day for over one hundred days. That meant a lot of cooking, cleaning, and feeding, and extra expense Mom and Dad could not really afford. Close family members were welcome of course, but the rest were just "kin folk." I think I learned to dislike Southerners that summer, and I'm not sure I'm over it yet.

Friends

I THINK A WORD OR two about my friends should be inserted here. I don't count but two friends my age until I was in the first grade…Claudia and George. But in the first grade I found someone who became my "best friend" for life. Yep, the same kid I first saw at the old laundromat. At first it was competition and fistfights, but Benny Nork and I finally became best buddies. We remained close friends until his death in a logging accident. He had just turned thirty-seven.

It was Benny and I who were thrown in the poison oak patch by two older kids, Myrtle Flowers and Richard Hess, and it was Benny and I who caught them one at a time and rubbed their bellies with the same poison oak.

Neither of us reacted to poison oak. Benny said it was because we chewed a poison oak leaf. When I told my mother about chewing a leaf, I wound up drinking and puking a gallon of dishwater. Still don't know if the dishwater or chewing the leaf prevented my reaction to the poison oak. I do caution those with curious minds to avoid experimentation with poison oak leaves, however.

Myrtle and Richard were both in need of a doctor shortly after we had our revenge. I wound up at Myrtle's house reading to her for an hour every evening for two weeks. Benny did the same for Richard. They recovered, but they were forever wary of the two of us after that.

Richard was prone to throw rocks, and once he hit me in the back. It hurt like the dickens. I picked up a nice round rock and threw it side-arm at him. Hit him right over his right eyebrow. Both of our mothers saw me throw that nice rock, but they didn't see him throw the first one, so I was the one in trouble…again.

Richard bled quite a bit before his mother staunched the bleeding, and that ended the rock wars in our neighborhood. I'll admit to feeling pretty bad about hurting Richard, but he was always starting something mean.

Dale Casey missed about half of our first year. I found out later in life he had a serious kidney problem. Anyway, Dale became my intellectual buddy. We both liked learning stuff, and when it came to science and math, we both "got it." After all these years, we are still good friends. We meet at least once a year at Diamond Lake to fish and to tell our "remember when" stories. Our friend Jim Vanderlip, who moved to Shady Cove along about the third grade makes it an annual threesome.

We had two Marions in our class. Marion Flowers and Marion David Walters, a tall, thin boy who was pretty quiet, at least according to my unreliable memory. Later in life he told my friend Dale he chose to go by his middle name, David, because the other Marion was a girl.

Dale tells me Marion Dave Walters felt a bit better about his first name after Dale told him John Wayne's first name was Marion. I have to smile at that.

I also became friends with Elden Elder, Jim Vanderlip's cousin, and a year older than us. All through my third grade Elden would walk the road from the Cove right past our house and out to the bus stop at the Post Office-store combination at the south end of the Shady Cove bridge.

One cold, frosty morning Mother spotted Elden walking the road in below the summer house. He wasn't wearing a jacket and he was about half an hour early for the bus. Mom said, "Go ask Elden if he wants some breakfast." The rest of the school year Elden was a frequent arrival, early enough to knock on the door and help me eat hotcakes or oatmeal for breakfast, and we became lifelong friends.

He was a radio listener and introduced me to pro football. He was a big fan of Johnny Unitas, and I remember going to Elden's house and listening to the games on the radio. Hooked me on football, he did. Or at least until all of those millionaire players started taking a knee to dis the American Anthem and the American flag.

Boy Scouts

Benny's mother, Marie, set up a cub scout pack. We'd meet at Benny's house, one of the few "modern" houses in shady cove at that time, and do cub scout things. I honestly can't remember what those "things" were any more, but I do remember it segued into boy scouts.

The neat thing about Boy Scouts was the unfinished cabin about half a mile up the hill from our house on Old Ferry Road. It was framed in, had a roof and a big rock fire pit right in the middle with a circular hood and chimney, but it was never finished so it was just an open-air structure. Nonetheless, it was a special place I visited often.

My memory says our scout troop only camped there once, and we didn't camp in the cabin. My first camp out meant packing a bedroll and some gear…skillet, hatchet, knife, a big T-bone steak and the rest…matches, salt. This was before I became a bit more of a minimalist when it came to backpacking. This first pack only weighed about sixty pounds.

The major point of this camp out was learning to cook over a camp fire. I did pretty well with my cast iron skillet and the steak, but my camp bread, water, salt, flour twisted around a willow stick, left something to be desired. I'll give myself a D- and tell you I never bothered to try it again.

Jim Vanderlip, Dale, Benny, Jake Stockwell, a new kid in our class, and I rounded up some rocks for a fire circle, laid out our bedding around the fire and told ghost stories. My memory says Jake was the only one who had a sleeping bag, which is important to this story.

We managed to spook ourselves with ghost stories like "Who's Got My Big Toe," when a coyote howled close enough to make the hair on my neck curl. Jake stood up and hopped his sleeping bag all the way around the fire and plopped down between Jim and me. We all had a good laugh over that.

Memory says Dale Goodman was our Scout Master, and he took us on several camp-outs, but we were never very good scouts. Once we earned out First-Class badge, we were too busy fishing the river and roaming the hills to do the other things required to be an Eagle Scout.

I still have my old Boy Scout Handbook, and I was tempted by a knot tying book at Barnes and Noble a few days ago. The title of the book was Knot Tying. Might go back and buy it and see if I can relearn my knot tying.

I'll just wrap this up by saying Boy Scouts was big in my young life. I have fond memories of a fishing trip to Four Mile Lake, a hike to Flounce Rock, a Boy Scout Jamboree, during which I whacked a finger with my pocket knife. I still carry the scar. I still live the Boy Scout Motto: Always Be Prepared.

I'm trying hard not to editorialize, but I fear we let NOW and other attack groups ruin a perfectly good organization.

One more story and I'll let this rest. A young woman who was apparently suffering from post-partum emotional problems, took her newborn and jumped from the Shady Cove bridge into the river.

The boy scouts were marshalled to scour the south side of the riverbank looking for mother and baby. Our friend Stanley Johnson, a year behind us in school found the woman's body. The baby was never found. I thought then and think so now it was a pretty rotten thing to foist on a twelve-year-old boy. But the culture at the time was "Life is hard and you had better get used it. Grow 'em up fast and kick 'em out at eighteen."

Television

We didn't have a TV station in the Rogue Valley until along about 1951, and then it was only one channel…Channel 5 in Medford. The men would gather at the home of whomever had the best reception and watch Friday Night Fights. Uncle Charles would tune the TV to the fight and then turn the sound off while he listened to the radio announcer call the fight. I remember there was some discrepancy between the radio description and what I could see on TV, but it was an interesting way to "watch" a boxing match.

Dad said TV was going to ruin the art of conversation. He was right, and I sometimes wonder what he would think now of the distraction of our cell phones and computers.

My parents weren't interested in actually owning a TV set. And they didn't until I was about twelve years old. And they didn't buy that one. Uncle Charles couldn't stand the fact we didn't have TV when he came to visit, so he brought an old set of his to the house and hooked it up. He ran the antenna wire under the living room window to the front porch and used the metal screen on the porch as an antenna so we could watch the news on Channel 5. Dad didn't say anything, but in truth he was a little pissed off about it. I don't remember what he said, but my father could cut you with a stare. There was no doubt in my mind what he was thinking. I will admit, however, to finding a lot of magic in TV programs.

We watched episodes of *Roy Rogers, the Lone Ranger, Gene Autry*, etc., and watched the news on a small and snowy black and white screen. But we didn't spend long evenings in front of the TV. We still played board games as a family: Chinese checkers, regular checkers, Monopoly—games like that. It was good family time and made it possible for my little sister Gloria to participate.

And Mom continued to listen to her radio programs—programs like *Fibber Mcgee and Molly, Young Widow Brown, The Bickersons, Sky King*…and a slew of other programs I don't remember very well. I listened to Buster Brown on Saturday mornings. One program I listened to when we were still living in the shack was about molecules. It explained why we couldn't move without the "space" in our molecules. That was an eye-opener. By gollies, I got it.

Note: Somehow, the fact that Gloria was born while Dad was in France and Germany, made her a special child, and Mom brooked no interference from Dad. Mom would halt any discipline of Gloria coming from Dad. As a consequence, Gloria would be an adult before she and Dad built any kind of father-daughter relationship. In his seventies, Dad would still talk about it during our hunting trips, trying to understand Mother's protective attitude towards Gloria. Maybe it would be more accurate to say trying to understand why Mom shut him off from being a father to his daughter. I don't think he ever worked out a satisfactory answer. I know I never did. And, of course, it is now too late to ask that question, even if I dared.

(My goodness, what a wandering tale. I'll try to straighten it out later… maybe.)

Heroes

My world was full of men who seemed to like kids, especially boy children, and as the first-born Collins grandchild I had special treatment, especially from Grandpa Truman Collins. He started a savings account for me, about one-hundred dollars as I recall, a lot of money in those days, and he gave me a heifer calf. I guess he gave me the heifer because subsistence living was a big part of our world. Maybe he figured a cow would be a help. Anyway, I grew up in the confidence I was the favored child, both a good and a bad thing to inflict on a boy.

I had uncles galore, Uncle Bill Walsh, Uncle Mendel Collins, Uncle Charles Hazelton, Uncle Darrel Troop, Uncle Cliff Troop, and Uncle Dean Collins. It was the habit in those days, maybe a holdover from the Missouri culture, to call older men "Uncle." So, I had several other uncles. One was Bob Frost, and it wasn't until I turned about twelve I found out he was Mom's first cousin and not an uncle at all.

But my all-time favorite was Uncle Dean, the youngest son of Opal and Truman Collins. He was just barely nine years older than me, I think, though Aunt Idelle may have to straighten me out about that. He was just my big brother, and from the time I was five, he packed me around with him. At age five, I shot my first squirrel with 4-10 shotgun, steadied over his shoulder while he knelt in the grass. I still have a picture in my mind of the big Silvergray coming down out of a tree.

I can't bring myself to kill anything these days, but five-year-old boys don't harbor any concern about killing squirrels. I went deer hunting and fished Reese Creek with him, followed him along the farm ditches while he checked his muskrat traps, "helped" him milk the twenty or so heifers on Grandpa's farm, and learned why I never wanted to have any beehives around my place. Those honeybees can sure sting a boy.

Dean did two other things for me. He taught me to hunt, and he taught me to box. He'd say things like, "Look at the shoulders on Rod." I got pretty puffed up, and during one visiting trip to the Eagle Point grade school with Dean when I was about five, a bigger kid pushed me down and I smacked him. He was a good twenty pounds heavier and a head taller, but I thought nothing of that. I was convinced I could whip him. Memory says he gave me a black eye. Maybe. Probably. But it didn't change my mind about how tough I thought I was.

Two of Dean's friends, Al Johnson and Floyd Berg sort of adopted me as well. It was more than just tolerate. They helped me kill my first buck, a chunky three-point blacktail. I was twelve years old when they put me on a "stand" and pushed that little buck right past me. I was a fairly good shot in those days, so I only missed him once. That unlucky critter stopped in a

The Collins family story of resilience, kindness. strength, and laughter

little clearing and I dropped him with my second shot. I was pretty puffed up when Dean, Al, and Floyd came hoofing out of the timber to my stand.

This might be a good time to confess I felt bad for the buck, but the culture of my world at that time made me push that feeling aside, and I went on to shoot quite a few more bucks before I hung up my deer rifle. And I will confess I didn't mind being the big cheese when I went to school the following Monday and told my friends the tale of shooting my first buck. But, again, I stray from the narrative.

Helping Hands

IN SPITE OF BEING DIRT poor during the first years of our return to Shady Cove, Mom and Dad found the motivation and resources to help other people. There were two women in town, both of whom were raising children, and both married to men who were gone for long months at a time, leaving their families without a thin dime for support. Both men were prospectors, one looking for uranium, the other looking for gold. I'll only say they were both cold-blooded sonsabitches to neglect their families in such a dismal way.

Several times Dad killed a deer (okay, maybe poached one) and left a haunch of venison hanging on each back porch. Mom would share jars of her precious canned salmon and canned fruit and canned green beans with those women. She would say, "People have to eat." Memory tells me potatoes cost one penny a pound, or one dollar for one-hundred pounds…so that became another of those helping foods from Mom and Dad.

Mom and Dad helped Elbert and Betty Hefley get a start in Oregon after they sold out in Southern California and joined us at the Holcomb place.

Dad got Elbert a job and taught him how to fall timber. The vernacular at time was "broke in."

They stayed with us at the Holcomb place through one winter and later moved into one of the two cabins Dad bought in Shady Cove the next spring. Within a few months, Elbert went to work for Medco (Medford Corporation) and then he and Betty bought a house on Reese Creek just above the old Pruitt store. They lived there until Elbert retired. I believe Floyd Berg, Uncle Dean's friend later bought that place from them.

For those that don't know the geography of the Rogue Valley: North from Medford on Highway 62 takes us to the Crater Lake Junction. Go east from there toward the town of Butte Falls. The first big bend in the road, a ninety-degree left takes us past the Collins farm on the east side of the highway, a hundred acres of irrigated land that grew enough hay to support a small dairy herd.

The last time I drove through there, the land was subdivided and had a couple of newer homes perched on what was once farm fields. The fields are neglected, full of weeds and woofy grass. The old barn out by the highway is still standing, but it has shrunk because it is a whole lot smaller than I remember. Neglected is another word that comes to mind. The upper pasture supports a pot farm. I think I'll take a drive through there on my next trip to Shady Cove.

""Uncle" Bob Frost, c. 1940

Bob and Marciel Frost also joined the ranks of family members Mom and Dad helped. Bob was the son of Frank and Edna Frost. Edna was Grandpa Troop's sister. When Bob and Marciel moved to Shady Cove along about 1947, housing was in short supply, so they started out in a tent cabin just down the street from our two shacks. A tent cabin was a deck, board walls about four feet high and rafters for a canvas roof. Primitive living is what it was.

Bob was a good equipment operator, thanks to the U.S. Army. During the War he had a lot of practice. His construction battalion landed on the Normandy beaches and fought across France and into Germany. He once told me the tale of his company chasing the German guards out of a concentration camp. The naysayers wouldn't be so sure there were never any concentration camps if they listened to Bob's story.

Bob and Marciel finally found a nice cabin upriver from Shady Cove at McLeod just above the present-day Casey State Park, not too far from the junction of the Rogue River and Butte Creek. There is nothing left now to indicate a small community ever existed at McLoed.

From there they moved to Oregon City. I'm not sure what Bob was doing for work at that time.

River Place

Before my ninth birthday, Mom and Dad bought a small two-bedroom, two-story house sitting on two acres of ground fronting the Rogue River. It wasn't exactly an upward move from the summer house, but we owned the place.

In the first year, water came to the house from the river via a pipe fed by an electric pump which had to be disconnected and moved to higher ground when the river flooded, but we had an electric water heater, flush toilets and a wringer washer. Heat came from a wood stove in the living room, and from the wood cook stove, until that was replaced by a modern electric range.

By the second year Dad had a well drilled and ended our dependence on river water. There weren't many houses above us and the folklore of the time said the sun and oxygen stirred into the water by riffles and rapids purified the water in a short distance.

I'm not sure about that, but I do have a tale about drinking margaritas in Guymas, Mexico, quite few years later. When I asked my friend Larry Ped who was hosting on the deck of the Hotel Ruby where he got the ice, he said, "From the fish house." Everyone got sick…except me. Maybe my immune system was toughened up from drinking river water.

It was along about this time that Mom bought her first electric stove. At times, especially at canning time, she bemoaned the loss of her wood cook stove because the wood stove had so much more cooking surface. But, on hot days the electric stove was a bit more pleasant.

Other events stand out in my mind:
- Dad bought a small cat and a log truck and started buying and logging small patches of timber while Clay Knotts ran their Shell

service station. The station was their source of wholesale fuel, tires and parts, and winter income. It was a good arrangement.

- Dad built a small barn which was floored with 12x12 beams (and which became part of another story a few years later).
- We camped at Hyatt Lake on June 5, my ninth birthday, and nearly froze in a snowstorm. We had more money by that time, but not much was spent on camping gear.
- Dad found me a good quarter horse named Shorty. I spent twenty-five dollars to buy him. It was money straight from the savings account Grandpa Collins set up for me.
- Bob Frost gave me my first rifle, a single shot Remington .22. It was a perfect gun for a kid. When you pulled the bolt back to load another shell, it automatically put the gun on "safe."
- To the best of my memory, Dad was the first to use hydraulic forks for loading logs on a truck. He was a good logger and we finally had enough money for some luxury items…if you can count a newer Ford as a luxury item, or a new couch for that matter.

About the barn: it was big enough for a calf pen with a side door that opened to a pen, a milking stanchion, and a loft that would hold about three tons of hay.

And it meant bringing Queeny, my small Guernsey milk cow from Grandpa's dairy farm on Reese Creek to our place.

It also meant milking the cow twice a day. Talk about being pinned down. Unless we could find someone who knew how to hand-milk a cow, we were stuck.

Note: Queeny spent her days as a calf with some free-range stock and it seemed to have bred a need for more room than the acre of pasture where she grazed. She'd jump the fence and just leave. More than once we paid a vet to stitch a teat cut by the barbs on the wire, and then spent days using a milking needle on her.

Old Shorty, a bay-colored quarter horse, was a perfect fit for a green rider. When I fell off, a frequent occurrence in the early days of my horseback riding, he just stopped and waited for me to get back on.

At first Dad said I could only ride bareback. No saddle. No chance of getting a foot caught in a stirrup and dragged to death. The only hitch in that bareback get-along was figuring out how to get my short nine-year-old body up on the horse. If I walked him up alongside a wooden box I used for a boost, he'd wait until I started to get on and then just sidestep.

I finally figured it out. I led him to the side of the barn and put my box on the outside. The barn kept him from swinging his butt away. Over time, like maybe in two months, I learned to grab a hank of mane and swing up on his back.

I won't bore you with details of my rides and the times I fell off except to say when I rode the hills, Shorty was prone to head for the lowest limb he could find and try to scrape me off. And he did run away with me, twice. Both times when we were headed for home. Those gallops brought tears to my ears, and I learned to appreciate his speed.

The Oglesby family had several big palomino horses they thought a lot of. And I will admit they were pretty with pale manes, yellow hair, just nice to look at. For some reason I can't remember, they rode their horses to our place. There was a five-acre field between our place and the Old Ferry Road. Memory says they started teasing me about my "little" horse.

Dad was grinning when I challenged them to a race. Given the short field, it was no contest. Shorty was a quarter horse and quick to start. Three times old Shorty and I were waiting at the end of the pasture for the bigger horses to get started.

By the time I was fourteen, owning a horse had turned from fun into a chore. Shorty, like the heifer, was prone to jump fences and pester the neighbor's orchard or step on the lid to their cesspool. We'd get a call and I'd go get my horse...again. We finally put him sort of "out to pasture" on the Flounce Rock Ranch where John Taylor worked as the ranch foreman, the same John Taylor that ran the cook house at Tiller Mill when I was about four years old. Once in a while John used Shorty when moving his cattle to new pastures. My horse was nearly thirty years old when he died. I don't think he ever missed me.

After all the trouble Shorty brought me, I know I never wanted to own another horse, although I think they are one of the most beautiful creatures on the planet. Their configuration is something special. It is easy to believe God created them for us to ride.

The Four Brothers

IF THIS WAS A COURTROOM, I'd say the judge called for a sidebar because I can't just leave the story of Shorty without recalling a mean event that almost ended in a shooting.

For starters, I should tell you I remember four brothers, all in their early twenties who dressed and acted like old-time gunfighters. They packed six-shooters in holsters, wore cowboy hats and cowboy boots, rode horses, and pretended to be the pure quill. I can't say from this distance and time if they were or not so I'll let that slide.

What I do know is they decided to round up the little bunch of wild horses running in the hills east of our place. And as luck would have it, Shorty jumped the fence again and wandered up on the hill above the house. When the cowboys, I'll be kind and give the brothers that honorific, started herding the wild horses, they managed to get Shorty inside their sweep of the hillsides. When one of the cowboys tried to head Shorty off, he just put his shoulder into the rider's horse and knocked him down.

It took them two or three days of hard riding to finally get about a half dozen horses into the old corral just across the road from our driveway. When they tried to rope Shorty, he put his head against a post. The rope wouldn't slide around his neck. And when they tried to slip the end of a rope around his neck, he bit them.

A neighbor kid, Lee Collingwood, an arch enemy of mine at the time, was watching the rodeo and told the cowboys the little bay was my horse. They sent someone to the house, so I went up to the corral, walked in and put a halter on Shorty and took him to our home pasture.

That should have put an end to the story, but I'm pretty sure Lee let those wild horses out of the corral that night. He and I were about the same size and he left a footprint.

The brothers decided I was the culprit, probably because old Shorty embarrassed them, so they came rolling up the drive to the house. Dad met them in the driveway. They said they intended to whip me. Dad stepped back into the house and grabbed the .32 Winchester Special from behind the door, stepped off the porch and jacked a round into the chamber. He assured them I had not let the wild horses out, and they sure as hell weren't going to beat on a twelve-year-old boy.

While that going on, I slipped out of the second-floor dormer window on the back side of the house with my .22 and laid on the ridge top for a rest. I took a bead on the driver because I sure has hell wasn't going to let them shoot my dad. I don't know what backed them off…Dad's cold eyes, the Winchester, or that dumb kid with the rifle. But back off they did, and with the strong assurance from my dad that if they ever came over on our side of the river again, he'd shoot first and talk later.

Dad didn't know I had backed him up until years later I confessed while we sat around the campfire in our hunting camp in Elkhorn Campground in the Maury Mountains. My confession scared the crap out of him. He spent a few minutes playing "what if?" He really didn't want to shoot those boys.

I heard a tale later in life that Dad's best friend, John Dickinson, looked the brothers up and assured them he'd shoot each one of them in the belly with his old colt .44 if they ever messed with me. I have no way of knowing if that was true, but at that time there was still a touch of the Old West in Shady Cove. And I can believe if John actually did brace them, it worked. John did not bluff about such things and when he was mad, he had the coldest eyes I've ever seen.

Gloria

IT OCCURS TO ME I neglect my sister Gloria in recounting our time in Shady Cove. What I remember about her is colored with a sense of her fear. She was intimidated by the cow, she was afraid of the horse, dogs scared her, and she was sick a lot. In looking back, I now realize she was probably allergic to milk, and may also have suffered from celiac disease. So, what did we drink and eat? Raw milk and Mom's baked bread, biscuits, cookies, cakes, or hot cakes made from white flour. Gluten free had not been mentioned in our world yet.

Our formal doctoring was seldom. Mother used home remedies most of the time. And mostly those worked or I wouldn't be here to write this tale. It also meant that diagnosis was casual and often wrong in the years we lived in Shady Cove. I can remember only two trips to a doctor for any illness: once when Gloria and I had terrible sinus problems, and once when Gloria had scarlet fever. Mom did take me to a doctor for a badly cut foot, for a broken nose I inflicted on myself while experimenting with a "new" way to high jump, and a bad cut on my left thumb when I was playing Tarzan and hacking my way through the jungle.

It is sad to say, but it seems likely a good doctor would have made the connection between Gloria's illnesses and a lactose intolerance, and maybe also a gluten intolerance. And my dear sister might have lived a few year years longer.

Marshal

I BELIEVE I WAS ELEVEN years old when a man I recall as "Marshal" was driving log truck for Dad and Clay Knotts, Dad's partner in the service station and in the logging outfit. At that time Clay was still running the Shell station they owned and had yet to go logging with Dad. Marshal had some kind of psychotic break and said he was going to kill my dad and the rest of us, and he was going to kill Clay and his family too. Dad took him seriously.

The Oregon State Police were called. They picked up Marshal and took him to jail. A judge reviewed the situation and told the State Police to take Marshal to the California/Oregon state line and dump him out. The judge also ordered him to never return to Oregon or he would face jail time. (I reckon the judge wasn't very understanding of mental illness.)

At any rate, Dad sat us down and told us what Marshal had said and what the State Police had done about it. So, we planned what we would do if Marshal showed up at the house. A loaded .32 Winchester Special was kept behind Mom and Dad's bedroom door. My job was to take Gloria down to the willows on the river and hide. Mom would defend the house.

At first I was thrilled. Mom would shoot the sonofabitch! And then I was scared to death, and I stayed that way for the next three years.

Even though I was only eleven, I could see great flaws in this plan. First, there was no way we could keep him from sneaking up on the place at night. Sandy, my little yellow mutt wasn't much of a watch dog, more likely to beat you to death with his tail than bark. Second, who would warn Mom if Marshal came to the house? When we were at school and Dad was off logging? Third, how would Mom get help? There were no phones lines yet on the Old Ferry Road where we lived. Nope. If he surprised her, it would be Katy-bar-the-door.

The Collins family story of resilience, kindness. strength, and laughter

I won't say fear ruled my life, but it was a constant companion. At night, unknown to my parents, I would load my .22 rifle and set it in the corner of my upstairs room, and then I would put my hunting knife under my pillow. Every night for almost three years. At daybreak, I'd unload the rifle and put my knife back in the sheath.

I became wary of any car I didn't recognize as local, and when I walked home after dark from the VFW Hall where we had our Boy Scout meetings, I'd walk the shoulder of the road and drop into the ditch and hide when a car came by. I won't say I was paranoid, but damned close.

I slept on the second floor of the house, and even in the hottest of weather, I never opened my window. I guess you could say I just sweated it out.

At the end of the second year after Marshal went bonkers, we were in Medford for some reason I can't recall. Dad gave me a dollar and sent me down a block to a burger stand that sold four good burgers for a dollar. I paid the man and was toting my bag of burgers up the street when I spotted Marshal. And there we were again.

Dad found a phone booth and called the police, and again Marshal was picked up. He was driven to the state line and kicked out all over again and told never to come back to Oregon. And, so, we lived under the threat of death for another year.

By the end of the third year, I had grown tired of being afraid, and one hot summer night I just unloaded my .22 rifle and hung it on the pegs on the wall, put my hunting knife back in the sheath and opened the window. The breeze felt fine. I turned my back on the window and got a good night's sleep for the first time in three years.

I learned several things from this. First, fear is not always rational. That's why I am very accepting of people who have phobias about various things. I still don't like high places. Shoot, I get the shivers just watching mountain climbing movies. Second, some threats need to be taken seriously. Third, you can overcome fear and keep it from crippling your life.

I'm not sure what happened to Marshal, but when we had to leave our place on the river, one good thing occurred to me: Marshal would not know where we lived.

As a boy I was afraid of all snakes, especially rattlesnakes. When I was about ten years old, I spotted a book in our school library about snakes. I checked it out and read all about Crotalus, the infamous rattle snake. That helped tame my fear a lot. There is something to be said about knowing your enemy. I'm still wary when I'm in rattlesnake country, but I know a lot about those particular critters and how to avoid them.

Time in the Clouds

YOU KNOW, I'D REALLY LIKE to write a straight-down-the-line recounting of our family history, but memories visit me totally out of sequence. For example, when we were still living in the summer house, Grandma and Grandpa Troop were, for a time, living in the trailer park across the bridge from our side of the river.

That was the summer I got fired from my very first job. The owners of the trailer park had a set of gas pumps out front. Tending that, working the little store and keeping the park cleaned up just didn't work out. So, they paid me thirty-five cents a day to sit out front and pump gas. That was the whole job, pump gas.

Think about that: child labor laws had not interfered with a kid's chance of finding a way to earn some money. Now, teenagers can't work until they are at least fifteen, and that's for fast food jobs. I keep thinking about Elden Elder who ran the jammer and loaded log trucks all summer when he was fifteen.

But back to the gas pumps. I can assure you there just wasn't a lot to occupy the attention of an eight-year-old boy in 1949. On a busy day, I might pump three or four tanks of gas. So, because I liked to read, I'd bring a novel. The only problem was my tendency to get so deep into the story I wouldn't notice when a car drove up. I'd just keep reading.

Finally, the owners of trailer park paid me my last thirty-five cents and said they wouldn't need me anymore. I don't remember needing to be told why.

I'm not sure I ever escaped the tendency to become engrossed in a book or in what I am thinking about. One of my jobs when we moved from the summer house to our own place was to feed the hogs Dad raised in a pen behind the barn. The house set about four hundred feet from the river. The barn set about half-way between the house and the river.

One fine Saturday morning, I guess I must have been lost in the clouds… again…because I wound up on the riverbank with two buckets of feed for the hogs. I had walked right past the pens and those noisy hogs without noticing them.

Another disconnected memory: Grandpa Charlie and Grandma Ida Troop lived in Brea, California, but his heart lived on the Rogue River, so along about 1948, they sold the Brea place and moved to Oregon.

Grandpa's retirement from Shell Oil wasn't all that much, so he worked as a janitor at the Talent high school. That was about when he was diagnosed with stomach cancer. All I'll say is he chewed tobacco for many years. Anyway, he had stomach surgery to remove the cancer. It didn't work, and he lived three hard years before he died.

But he and I shared days on the river. I'd sneak up on him, always barefoot, nearly silent in the sand, and hear him chuckling. It almost always meant "fish on." He'd unhook the fish, and if the fish wasn't hurt, he'd turn it loose. Then he'd say to himself, "Well, we know that works. Let's try something else."

I think his last trip with us was to Hyatt Lake. Grandma and Grandpa Troop, my cousin Terry, Dad and I crowded into an old eighteen-foot wood drift boat Dad found someplace.

Hyatt Lake was a reservoir we fished quite few times each year. When the dam flooded the meadow, no one bothered to clear the trees out. So after the trees died and the bark slid off, it was like a ghost lake, lots of white, dead snags sticking up, buckskin logs floating in the water, perfect crappie and bass water.

We had an old green Evinrude outboard to push the boat, but we used oars in and around the snags and logs. Grandma wanted to fish off of a log she picked out. So I rowed her in. Grandpa helped her get out and I backed the boat away, just before the log began to sink. It was a big log, but it was so waterlogged it wouldn't support her.

Grandpa was laughing and Dad was shouting at me to get the boat back over to her. She was chest deep before I could get the boat backed to her log. Dad was pretty miffed at me until Grandma got to laughing. Thank goodness. That took me off the hook.

Between the five of us, we caught maybe 150 crappie, all lined up on a cotton stringer. As dark sneaked up on us, Dad said, "We should go in while we can still see the bank."

With that, he pulled the crank on the old Evinrude outboard. Danged if it didn't start on the first pull, probably the first and only time it ever did. The boat picked up speed before I could get the fish into the boat, and sure enough, the old cotton stringer broke. I hollered and Dad turned us around. Occasionally we'd spot a dorsal fin on the dark water, but we lost all the fish anyway.

Terry and I fumed, and Dad and Grandpa and Grandma all laughed at our fussing. I remember Dad saying something like, "Well, we won't have to clean all those fish, and we had the fun of catching them."

I think we humans make a big to-do out of the "last this" or the "last that" when we should celebrate the time instead. Yes, that was the last time I fished with Grandma and Grandpa Troop, but it was a great trip, full of laughter and fun. I still have a clear picture in my mind of the log sinking under Grandma Ida while she held the pole up and out of the water. I remember her laughter at the predicament.

That said, it jogs another memory of Grandpa taking me fishing on a pier that jutted out into the Pacific. I was about four. Don't hold me to this, but memory says it was in Huntington Beach. This was during the war when Dad was in Europe. Grandpa sort of looked out for me from time to time. Good thing, too. I just wasn't cut out for neighborhoods.

But back to Shady Cove. When I was twelve, Uncle Dean finished his time in the Navy and came home to Oregon. But he brought a wife with him. I had a hard time with that. Like all kids, I was born a conservative. I liked things the way they were, and I didn't cotton to change.

Here was my "big brother" uncle with a strange woman in tow. I was staying with Grandma and Grandpa Collins for a few days at their house in Butte Falls when Dean and Idelle drove up. (If my memory is correct, a year or two after Dean left the farm for college…and then a two-year stint in the Navy, Grandpa Collins sold the farm, and moved to Butte Falls.)

Somehow Idelle understood my distaste for this marriage business, and we wound up sitting in the living room and talking until midnight. We have remained friends since, and I made my peace with another of life's adjustments.

Within a short time Dean and Idelle moved into a small house in Shady Cove. He worked a while for a surveyor. As most of us who ever did that kind of work, he liked it. I once worked two weeks brushing and pulling chain and pounding hubs. Great job!

Me and my shadow. Dean and Idelle's first house is in the background. 1955

Within a year he was working for Cascade Wood Products in sales. He was very good at his job, and he eventually wound up owning the mill after a few years. I do have a story of how that all came about, but I think I'll let Idelle and her brood tell it.

Dad owned five acres between our house and the Old Ferry Road. Dean bought the ground and started building a house. He was a meticulous builder and remained so for the rest of his life. He was more of an engineer than a carpenter.

I got to help him once in a while. When the foundation of his new home was being poured, the concrete was mixed in a gas-powered mixer and then dumped into wheelbarrows, which we pushed up a ramp to fill the foundation forms. I've forgotten the formula for the mix, but it was x shovels of gravel, x shovels of sand, and x shovels of dry cement. I can tell you it was a lot of work mixing and hauling the concrete to the forms. And you could not stop.

The whole foundation had to be poured in a couple of hours. As I recall, John Dickinson, Dean, Dad, Al Johnson and I were the entire crew.

Dean and Idelle built most of the rest of the house. I think about it from time to time. Dean was maybe 23 years old…and building his own house. Forest Dean, their first born was about a year old, and they would sit him in a stroller while they worked.

One cold winter day, Dean started a warming fire from scrap wood and backed up to the fire. He set his coveralls on fire and badly burned his leg. That one made for a trip to Medford where our closest doctor worked at that time.

It wasn't much later that Doc Loeffler set up a retirement practice at his house upriver from Trail. He stitched my thumb once and straightened my broken nose on another occasion.

All told, Dean and Idelle built three houses on that piece of ground Dad sold them. Grandma Opal bought one, and Dean and Idelle lived in a bigger house they built.

An old blacksmith bought the third house. The story goes that Wachang Metal in Albany sent two college educated metallurgists to visit him. Rumors were he had learned to work tungsten in an open forge. I believe he could because I have one of the knives he made. For us laypeople, working tungsten means a forge without oxygen…because raw tungsten will burn when exposed to the air. I don't know the outcome of their visit, but he continued to work metal in his open forge for sometime after that visit.

Logging

Dad's partner in the service station, Clay Knotts did not want to run the station while Dad had all the fun and made a heck of a lot more money than the service station brought in. Clay could not see the sense in having a good bread and butter business to carry them through the winter…one which gave them a source of wholesale gas, parts, tires, etc.

Reluctantly, Dad agreed to sell the station. They worked pretty well together. Clay drove truck and fell a few "sticks" while Dad loaded the log truck, an old REO they bought. It was a small outfit, and they would only get about 10,000 board feet a day to the mill. But peeler logs were worth about $90 per thousand board feet and saw-timber was worth about $40 a thousand. Even on a bad day, the operation grossed a decent profit and fed both families.

It wasn't long after Dad started logging that he bought a good car…a 1951 Ford sedan, a much-needed improvement over the 1941 Ford we drove until then. And Mother's new wringer washer meant no more trips to the laundromat.

The telephone company finally put a line up the river along the Old Ferry Road, the road to our place, and with the TV Uncle Charles brought us, we moved into the "modern" era. I tried that business of talking on the phone with my friends, but I wasn't very good at it. Just couldn't keep a conversation going. And I don't know if I'm much better these days. Sometimes, especially now during the Governor Kate Brown lockdown (2020-2021), I make a list of things to share when I call old friends. And since we've all gotten older and aren't doing a heck of a lot, it's a pretty puny list.

John Dickinson and his brother Dick owned a small cat and a log truck. John got a contract with a big company to clean up the spring salvage up on the Pea Vine Road west of the summit of the Tiller-Trail divide. John and John decided to work as partners on the Pea Vine job. It was good, big peeler timber, the roads were all in, and the landings were dozed out and graveled. All a logger had to do was move in after snowmelt, buck logs and start loading trucks.

Peeler logs were those used to make plywood. The mill actually peeled the wood into thin sheets called veneer by turning the big logs over and over against big lathes. The veneer was glued and pressed into sheets. The laminating made it much stronger than boards of the same thickness.

John Dickinson and my dad worked well together, so the partnership was successful. But they made a mistake. They would send the last load down the highway, load their gear up and head for the Trail Tavern for a cold beer. Unfortunately, they often passed the truck hauling the last load. And it irritated the heck out of Clay or Dick, who still had to drive to the mill in White City.

Both Clay and Dick were a little short sighted. John and John did all the heavy work, limb and buck the logs, set the chokers, skid and load the logs. All Clay and Dick had to do was drive truck. Period. One special week, the outfit cleared…after expenses…$8,000. At the time, you could buy a large farm for that much.

Their bellyaching finally got to Dad. He developed an ulcer and lived on Gelusol tablets. John Dickinson finally said, "Let's sell out and you and I partner and just fall timber for Red Blanket Lumber." And so that ended my father's days as owner of a logging outfit.

The Divvy

When their partnership broke up, Dad and Clay sold the cat, which left a pickup and the log truck, about four power saws, chokers for skidding logs, and an assortment of gas cans, and the other miscellaneous tools of logging.

Clay could not make up his mind on how to divvy this stuff. So Dad put two saws, and two gas cans, and an axe or two and set them in the back of the pickup. Then he told Clay that was one half and the truck was the other half. Dad told me one time around the campfire that Clay, who was almost twenty years older than Dad, had a tough time choosing, but as Dad figured he would, Clay chose the truck.

John and Johnny as they came to be known, tried to partner with John's brother Dick Dickinson, but according to John, Dick waited until John and my dad shut their power saws off, and then he'd fire his up to make it sound like he was working. So, once again, John Dickinson said, "I'm tired of carrying Dick. Let's not work with him anymore."

Dick had a tough time making a living after that. After his son Patrick was killed on the last day of Patrick's summer job working in the woods, Dick just drank his life away. He died from lung cancer at age 40. (The Eagle Point high school yearbook was dedicated to his son Patrick the year after Patrick was killed.)

So John Dickinson and Johnny Collins had about three happy years falling timber. One time a man asked the bullbuck (think "foreman") for Red Blanket Lumber how many sets of timber fallers he had. He replied he had just one set. The man said you can't put out that many loads with just two timber fallers.

The bullbuck said, "John and Johnny are my timber fallers. The other sets are my wood butchers."

Friends

I REMEMBER EIGHT YEARS OF grade school as one of occasional fist fights, best buddies and great teachers. My closest friend was Benny Nork. We just sort of knew what the other was thinking.

Dale Casey was my intellectual friend. We got the math and science part of life. And we both loved geography. But we were always in competition, so there were occasional fights. Once he threw his baseball bat as I was walking away from an argument. The bat hit me behind the knees, dropped me to the ground, and hurt to the point I couldn't chase him. So, I turned his bat label-side-up and broke it over the concrete steps. Dad made me give Dale my bat. To this day, I don't know why. Dale started it.

Jim Vanderlip joined our class in the third grade. He was a fun-loving kid, easy to get along with and a heck of a lot better athlete then he knew. From the seventh grade on, I was confident I could outrun any kid in school. Once, just once, Jimmy outran me. Sort of humbled me without knowing it.

Jim Vanderlip with his coonskin cap and fly rod

When we were in high school, I saw him press 135 pounds with one arm. And he only weighed 135 pounds at that time. Pound for pound, he was one of the strongest men I ever knew. Jim and Elden were cousins. I think. Never did get that part straight. I'll have to remember to ask Jim about that on our next fishing trip.

Kenny Williams was in our class off and on depending on which relative he was living with at the time. We were good friends, but he was always a bit distant. I think that might have been because he had no true home. When his sister married Dale Winkle who had a small farm up Indian Creek, the sister took Kenny in, and it seemed to work out better for Kenny until Dale was killed in a car wreck on the first corner upriver from Shady Cove. I'm pretty sure one of the Stockton brothers was driving, and I'm pretty sure they had been partying, but it probably worked better for all concerned if they said Dale was behind the wheel.

After that, Kenny lived with his dad for a spell. Kenny did not call him "Dad." Just called him "Hoot." That pretty well sums up Kenny's life through his childhood. He died a young fifty-five years old. I won't speculate as to why he had a heart attack at that age, but he did consume a fair amount of alcohol and he smoked from the time he was about fourteen. Those habits can be hard on a person. Maybe as hard as heartbreak and loneliness.

Doug Nork

WE WERE ABOUT SEVEN YEARS old when Benny's little brother Doug was killed in an accident on the log landing where Big Ben was moving equipment. As I remember the story, some seventy-plus years later, Big Ben had Benny and Doug stashed in a safe place, but when a tree broke, it scared Doug, and he ran down the log he was on and right under the tree. I think he was about five at the time.

As I think about Big Ben's logging career, he made his millions, but it cost him two of his three sons. Benny was killed in the woods at age 37, and it cost Big Ben a leg when two logs rolled together. And son Steve, Benny's younger brother was badly injured while falling timber. That's a heavy price to pay, including his marriage. I believe his wife Marie never get over the loss of Doug.

When Benny came to school a few days after the accident, we huddled in the school yard…Dale, Benny, Kenny and me…and tried to get a handle on what being dead meant. Didn't even get close, but we cried together a bit even though we tried hard not to.

Teachers

I WAS BLESSED THROUGHOUT MY school career with fine teachers, from grade school to high school and on to college. I won't try and rank one over the other, but Agness Brown was my favorite in grade school. She arranged to be our teacher four out of the eight years we were in Shady Cove Grade School. She was tiny, but she was strict. She would swat the palm of your hand with a rule. ("They are rules, not rulers," she would say.) I was in the eighth grade when she swatted me with a "rule" for the last time. It didn't hurt much, and I had to turn away to keep from laughing. (I didn't want to embarrass Missus Brown.)

I'd be remiss not to mention Bill Croucher who was our basketball coach and our sixth-grade teacher. He was a fine teacher and taught me the basics of geography, a subject I still enjoy. And we did place 3rd in the Rogue Valley grade school tournament. Earned a trophy and everything…even if we were the shortest team in the contest.

Mister Croucher told us to each pick a country of the world and work up a map. I chose Russia, and my map was carved on a pine board. I don't know what ever happened to it, but it marked the mental picture of Russia that I hold in my mind today, from the Caucus Mountains to the Bering Strait.

Me, Frank Petersen in grade school, c. 1955, although Frank was from another school.

I think Mister Croucher liked me. One opening day of fishing season, he took me fishing up on Muir Creek, just shy of where it feeds into the upper Rogue River. We didn't catch sick 'em, but I had a fun time, and I felt pretty special.

Then there was Missus Briggs. I'll never forget her lessons in hygiene. I think her notion of washing hands was a good one. Told us all about a world just packed with germs waiting to kill us.

She lectured us about picking our noses. Told us it would stretch our noses out and make us look ugly. And she was definitely against belching. Told us we would reach a point at which we could not control it. As for passing gas, you can imagine the picture I had in my mind about that.

Still, all things considered, she was a pretty nice person, except for the time we made paper mâché and were supposed to shape an animal from it. I was pretty proud when I showed her my frog. I still remember how I felt when she took a look at it and said it looked like the paper mâché was ready to shape now. By gollies, was she so blind she couldn't see the frog?

Baby Dean

I THINK I WAS ABOUT ten years old when Mom and Dad agreed to look after a foster child. I never knew his last name. He was always just Baby Dean. He was the victim of a bitter custody battle, and child services was pretty certain his mother was neglecting him and abusing him with spankings. He was three and still wetting his pants, and when he did, he would shake and cry and try to hide in a corner of the room or behind a door. That happened within the first hour of his stay with us.

It was obvious he got a licking every time he wet his pants. Mom calmly picked him up, shushed him gently, changed his diaper and cleaned him. He wasn't used to kindness, I think.

Over the three months he stayed with us, he gained about fifteen pounds, slept like "a baby" and calmed down. He was also potty trained by then.

His father won the custody battle, as he deserved to. When he came to the house to take Baby Dean home, it was a happy day for Baby Dean and a damned sad one for us. Gloria and I came to love the little guy, and while we understood he should be with his loving father, we felt like we had a lost a little brother. At least I did. Mom went for a walk down by the river, and

Gloria and I went to our rooms for the afternoon. I still wonder how life treated Baby Dean after that.

Stillborn

I THINK I MIGHT HAVE been about eleven or maybe twelve when Dad drove Mother to the hospital in Medford, the big town in our part of the world. Nothing much was ever said about it until Dad mentioned it years later. I was in my fifties by then. He told me Mother delivered a fully formed baby boy, but it was stillborn. I think they grieved silently for the rest of their lives.

The River

As I REREAD THE PREVIOUS pages, I think I might be painting a pretty grim picture. I'm sorry about that. There were grim times, but my growing up years on the river were idyllic. My bamboo fly rod leaned against the wall on the back porch, rigged up and ready for the next evening of fly fishing. Even when the river was closed to fishing, my fly rod still leaned against the wall on the back porch, along with my dad's. We never took them down.

Left to right: Leah, Terry, me, and Mike chunking rocks in the Rogue

In the off times, both Dad and I tied fishing flies. I got good enough to sell six dozen Royal Coachman fishing flies to Wally Crank at the Shady Cove Market. Seventy. Two. Tedious. Flies. I've never tied a Royal Coachman since. I don't intend to. I cussed myself after the first dozen. But I filled the contract.

The river ran from my right to my left, and after several years of fishing, the limber bamboo tip had a permanent left-handed crook in it, set there by the pressure of the current on the flyline.

In the summertime, the only question was whether to fish upriver from our place or downriver on a flat stretch of riffles that ran for a quarter mile in below our place.

One summer I waded the riffles and built piles of rocks in a staggered, off-set fashion as fish habitat. It worked. When the shadows covered the river, Dad and I frequently fished the riffles. We'd skip sections to leave fresh water for each of us.

I remember a big cottonwood log which shed all its bark over time. A flood floated the log in and jammed it between two big trees. That was the rendezvous point after the fishing was done. Dad and I would count the fish in our creels, and then sit on that old log and talk a bit while the mourning doves started their evening call, and the bats worked the river for insects. I tried hard to out fish Dad, but it seemed like he always had his limit of ten fish, and I was always shy of a limit by a fish or two.

Years later we packed a big eighteen foot two-person kayak into a place called Dinger Lake to fly fish for brook trout. I set up on the back of the kayak and paddled parallel to the old creek channel in the lake while he caught brookies that ran about twelves inches each. That's when I finally figured out how he always caught more fish than I did. His reflexes were a heck of lot faster than mine. He could set the hook before I even saw the fish.

On Dinger Lake, he was fishing a Rogue River special with a lead fly and a dropper fly, and sometimes catching two at a time. He finally stopped and asked if I wanted a turn. I remember smiling and saying, "Sure. We only need five more fish for our limit." The limit was still ten fish a day back then.

Growing up on the river meant a lot of fresh caught trout for dinner. Trout cooked by my mother always tasted better than any I have ever been able to cook. Maybe it was the lard and the cornmeal she used.

The Miserable Cow

As I wrote earlier, my grandfather, Truman Collins gave me a heifer calf when I was about five. The customs of the time called for naming each critter on a farm, so she was called Queeny.

I have no idea why, but when we moved into the "new" house on the river, someone, Grandpa maybe, brought her to our place. Dad built a tidy small barn that held about three tons of hay in the loft, had a milking stanchion, a calf pen and an area for feed and buckets and other paraphernalia of cow milking and calf raising.

There was a one-acre pasture to the river off the end of the barn. Water for the cow, a little space to wander and a dose of oats at milking time, plus a pillow of alfalfa each day seemed the right formula for a happy cow. The problem was she jumped fences. Dad thought her early years of life with cattle on a grazing allotment might have ruined her as a domesticated milk cow.

Inevitably, she would tear a tit on the barbed wire and Dad would send for the vet. That tit had to be drained by a milking needle for a few weeks, and then it was life back to normal…for a while.

The little heifer produced about four and a half gallons of milk a day, more than any four-person family could possibly use. So we fed some to a calf and two hogs, and Mother sold milk to the neighbors…seventy-five cents a gallon, and made butter, buttermilk and cottage cheese. It was a seven-days-a-week operation.

Dad was then working the service station seven days a week from about four a.m. to nine p.m. at night, so Mom and I did the milking. I was soon convinced if you own one milk cow, you might as well own a herd, because you were as tied down by one as you would be by a dozen. Cows have to be milked each morning and each evening seven days a week. Otherwise, they dry up. We tried to find a neighbor who could and would milk for us, but that was a rare event.

As fortune would have it, Grandpa Charlie had a heart attack on a visit to Southern California, so Mom, Gloria, and I headed for California to see him. We were gone about two weeks, and when we drove back into our yard, the cow was missing. (I have no idea why Grandpa Charlie was in California at the time. Visiting Aunt Juanita and Uncle Charles maybe.) At any rate, Dad was stuck milking Queeny.

As he told it, Dad closed the service station and was having a beer at the Rogue River Lodge, upriver a short distance from the little town of Trail. When a fella said he was looking for a milk cow, Dad said he had one for sale. They agreed on a price, but the sale was contingent on the man picking up his new milk cow before milking time the next morning.

I think we were all relieved to see old Queeny go. I know I was. Like a lot of critters we had over the years, she was just contrary and cantankerous. More trouble than she was worth, maybe, but I can still imagine the thick rich cream I poured on my breakfast cereal.

A Fish Tale

I READ A LOT OF novels as a kid, westerns, sailing stories, true crime, but for a time I was drawn to jungle tales. The Amazon was especially romantic in my mind. So I would cut willow poles and shape them into spears. I'd even heat the head to harden it like it was described in books I'd read. (I'm still not sure that helped. In fact, I'm pretty sure it doesn't help at all. You have to read novels with a grain of salt.)

After a spring flood of a minor sort, my dog Ted, a shaggy black and white something or other we called a "water spaniel" and I were prowling the river in below the house. Ted disappeared in a thicket of willows down along the riverbank. And then he started barking.

I pushed through to find Ted chasing a salmon in a backwater pool. It was a nice, big, bright fish we later weighed in at seventeen pounds. When the level of the river dropped back to normal, the fish was stranded.

I wadded into the pool, willow spear in hand, and chased the fish to the lower end where it beached itself on some sand. I pounced and speared the fish which put up enough tussle to break my spear. I reached for a rock and smacked it on the head…several times. When it quit twitching, I slung the fish over my back and took it home.

Mother was hanging out her washing when she spotted me. She laughed at the sight of her young son and his wet dog coming up across the field with a salmon in tow. When she asked how I'd caught the fish, I told her I'd speared it.

The Collins family story of resilience, kindness. strength, and laughter

I'll finish this tale by just saying we ate fresh salmon that night. A cautionary note: it wasn't fishing season, and spearing fish was and still is against the law. So don't you be doing that.

The Hills

I THINK I'VE NEGLECTED TO orient my future readers to the geography of Shady Cove. From the little town of Trail about two miles north of Shady Cove (both Trail and Shady Cove unincorporated at that time) the river runs mainly north to south until it reaches the Cove. At that point, the river hooks west for a distance of maybe a half mile before turning a slow half circle and heading south again.

Most of the homes and businesses sat along Highway 62 west of the river. Our house sat east across the river from town. As a kid it meant I had very few summer companions. So, I fished the river and hiked the hills in behind the house on Bureau of Land Management land. That area is roughly ten miles by ten miles…although it isn't exactly square. That was my playground, a place I searched for caves, looked for wild horses, chased squirrels, and learned to whistle like a Mountain Quail. And where I occasionally filled my buck tag.

When my chores were finished on Saturday morning, I was free to do whatever I wanted. No more chores or "have to" for the rest of the weekend.

On quite a few Saturdays I'd grab my .22 and a box of shells, and my hunting knife, stuff some prunes in a jacket pocket, some wooden matches, a bit of salt twisted in a piece of waxed paper, and a snake bite kit in the other pocket, and head for the hills. Now this predates cell phones. So the plan ran like this: if I got caught out and night was coming on, I was to keg up and wait for morning because Dad didn't want me to walk off a cliff in the dark; if I was hurt, I was to build a smudge fire so he could locate me. Most of the hills in behind the house were visible from our field or from the highway across the river.

That isn't true any longer. The trees have grown some in the past sixty plus years, so the view of the hills is a little more obscure. And the field I toted the salmon across back to the house is filled with homes and trees. I think I grieve over that a bit. Mother and Gloria hunted arrowheads in that big field.

After Bob Frost gave me the Remington single shot .22 rifle, I was king of the hill. Dad would not let me hunt with any other kids until I was twelve, so I'd load up and go exploring alone.

As I think about the freedom I had as a boy, I feel a little pinched by all the rules our politicians seem to need, and by all the people that have come to build on my fields, and who crowd my solitude. Shoot…you have to make reservations a year in advance to have space in a crowded campground.

Long Beach

At the end of my tenth summer, Aunt Juanita, Uncle Charles, Terry, Leah and Linda drove up from Long Beach, California, a long, slow nine-hundred miles, for a visit. As I recall, Terry and I slept out in a nice pup tent he made in Boy Scouts.

We were anxious for the sun to set so we could get on with our sleep out. It was pretty snug in the tent, and I was a little jealous because I didn't have one. We spread blankets and tucked in. When I rolled over something started buzzing. To my ears it sounded like a rattlesnake. And it was right in front of the tent. Scared the crap out of me.

I told Terry to get ready, and when I told him to, he was supposed to pull the tent flap back and I would jump out and run to the house for help. So I got in a runner's stance and Terry jerked the flap back. Barefoot, in my shorts, I sprinted to the house and got Dad and Uncle Charles. Armed with flashlights, we hurried back to the tent. Terry had pulled the flap back and was huddled at the very back of the tent.

Dad and Uncle Charles searched the tent first, and then the area around it. No snake, but Terry and I gathered up our blankets and followed the men back to the house. Sleeping out had lost its appeal.

The next morning Terry and I went back down to the hump where we had camped, about halfway to the river, to pack up the tent. We found a big pine beetle about two inches long. That was the critter imitating a rattlesnake. Made me feel a bit better about getting spooked. Those pine beetles make a sound that is a pretty good imitation of the buzz from a rattlesnake.

I think the Hazeltons stayed about a week. Sometime during that week, Juanita and Charles offered to take me back to California with them. Dad and Mom thought the world of Shady Cove was a bit narrow and I might benefit from a larger perspective.

I honestly can't tell you how I felt. But I loved being with Terry. So I didn't put up too much fuss. The plan was to attend grade school through the first term and then go back to Shady Cove in time for Christmas.

I can tell you I encountered a foreign world. For starters, the sun didn't have much poop. Smog was the order of the day. And I was totally lost outside the neighborhood. I worried about not being able to find my way home, either to the Hazelton house or back to Oregon.

Uncle Charles had a newfangled TV, the first I had seen, and I was mesmerized by the Lone Ranger, Roy Rogers and the whole Western gang. When they first turned it on after our long trip, I know I just sat and grinned like an idiot.

I also remember the new kids in the grade school weren't exactly friendly. I was a fifth grader and during recess two sixth graders told me that Oregonians weren't very tough. (I'll just remind my readers about Uncle Dean, learning to box and the advice he gave me before I started first grade. If someone wants to fight, don't talk. Just hit 'em. The first punch generally wins the battle.)

So I didn't say anything to these schoolyard toughies. I just smacked both of them...a left and then a right. Dean was correct. I didn't throw another punch, and the other kids left me alone the rest of my days there. I can't remember the name of the grade school, but I don't think it matters much to this story.

In those days, if you didn't draw blood, a schoolyard fist fight didn't mean a trip to the principal's office. You fought, and then shook hands and it was over.

Three events stick in my mind:
- Aunt Juanita took Leah, Linda, Terry and me to downtown Los Angeles on the train. We had a nice meal in a very famous restaurant, the Brown Derby maybe. I was awestruck. The fanciest place I had ever been to was a Chinese restaurant in Medford. (Can't remember the name of that place either. It'll come to me and I'll stick it right in the middle of something else.)

- Uncle Charles had a landscape business which included the grounds around the Coliseum. Terry and I helped one Saturday, raking leaves and pulling weeds. Our reward was a ticket to the Coliseum that same afternoon for a pro football game between the Los Angeles Rams and the Green Bay Packers. We were seated a long way from the field, but we were on the 50-yard line anyway. LA tromped Green Bay something like 35 to 6. Hooked me on pro football. For years I was a Rams fan.
- A boy in my class in Long Beach wrote a story about Indians. The teacher had him read it. I was astounded, and I remember it as a good story. I think it increased my desire to become a writer.

In early December Aunt Juanita helped me pack up, and Uncle Dean came by. We were driven to a bus depot someplace, climbed aboard a big Greyhound Bus and headed for Oregon. It was a long, cold, miserable trip. For starters, the bus wasn't heated, and north of Sacramento the night cooled off. I had on a light sweater and that was it. And, I had to pee but we were on an "express" which made few stops. Dean finally asked the bus driver to find a place to let me out. The driver stopped at the Greyhound Bus Depot in Dunsmuir, told everyone to stay on the bus and unlocked the depot door so I could use the bathroom. I can tell you I did not wet my pants, but it was a close thing.

Mom and Dad met us at the Medford Bus Depot in Medford. I did not cry, but my relief at being home was so great it was a close thing. And the sight of our house on the river made it the best Christmas ever.

Lessons:
- Missus Brown had us about a year ahead of the California kids. So I found the lessons boring.
- Nobody in their right mind should live in that smog choked place, and I wasn't anxious to ever go back.

I'll finish by saying, if memory serves, the Hazeltons moved to Talent, Oregon, the next school year. I haven't been to Talent since the Almeda fire in 2020, so I don't know how much of the town is left.

Russians

I sometimes think the threat of the A-bomb gets overlooked as it influenced my generation. We practiced ducking under our desks in case the Russians bombed us. And we had classroom films showing the devastation of Hiroshima and Nagasaki.

Once when I was about eleven about thirty B-17s bombers flew over Shady Cove at a low level and scared the crap out of me. (I've always had a bright imagination.) I don't know where they were going or why they were so low in the sky, but the roar of that many B-17s practically shook the ground.

I had nightmares after that about the Russians bombing Shady Cove. I know…rationally…no one would have wasted an ordinary bomb on Shady Cove, let alone an A-bomb. But fear is not rational.

After one very vivid dream I still remember, I started writing a story about a Russian invasion, and how my buddies and I took to the hills and fought a guerrilla war. The title was Ambuscade. And somehow that gave me control over the nightmares and my irrational fears. By, gollies there really was something I could do about those damned Russians.

Aside: I finished the novel during my senior year in high school. I'd scribble out a chapter and my good buddy Nancy Albin would type it up. It would make the rounds, and then I'd write another chapter. Several classmates wanted to know if they could be in my book. I always said, "'Sure." After all, it was a war book with a cast of thousands. Sometime in my sophomore year of college I dug it out and decided the quality of the writing was wanting, a lot, so I tossed the whole thing. When I saw the film Red Dawn, I thought, "Heck, I already wrote that one."

Back To Shady Cove

Shady Cove was a rough town when I was growing up. We didn't have a policeman closer than Medford some twenty-two miles south. And we had a reputation of being outlaws. The upside was the freedom to poach a deer when you needed meat, or snag a salmon when you needed one. The downside was the inability to get a bank loan to build a house if you had a Shady Cove address.

It pretty much stayed that way until 1964 when two warring families (and their friends) got into a drunken, bloody brawl at the Trail Tavern. That dust-up left ten men injured and needing medical care, and one man with severe brain damaged that he never recovered from.

Some had broken limbs. Logging chains and axe handles can do that. My memory says a couple of the brawlers wound up in the State pen.

The brawl was severe enough to make the national news. I was sitting in the cab of my Forest Service pumper truck, watching a lightning storm from the North Warner View Point northeast of Lakeview, sixty down strikes in thirty minutes, when the news came over the radio. I remembered some of the surnames from my childhood. After that, the Jackson County Sheriff stationed a deputy in Shady Cove. The deputy was known as a fair man, but tough on lawbreakers. And he lived very close to town. Law and order had come to Shady Cove a century after the first settlement.

The Raccoon

I THINK WAS ABOUT TWELVE and when Jim and Elden came to the house to explore the hills with me. We wandered up past Tommy Tucker's place and uphill from there, following a game trail that ran up the bottom of the canyon. We heard a strange noise coming from a deep cavity in a big oak tree.

Elden was tall enough to peek down the hole. He said something about an old raccoon caught in a trap. We decided it wasn't too darned nice to set a trap in a hollow tree. It was obvious the raccoon had been there a while and had been gnawing on the trapped leg because it was just hanging by tag of skin.

We took pity on the critter and decided to take it out so we could turn it loose. We dumped our coats in on top of the raccoon and Elden reached in and pulled him out. When he bit Elden, Elden dropped him on the ground, trap and all and put a foot on the critter to hold him still. Jim and I pried open the jaws of the trap. We were each rewarded with a bite from that desperate animal. It managed to slice open the tips of the four fingers on my left hand. I don't remember where Jim got bit. I'll have to ask him next time I see him.

That should have ended it, but we decided that old raccoon needed some food and water before we turned him loose.

Elden got his hand around the neck of the animal from behind and in front of its paws. That worked pretty well as long a I held the back legs. It was about a half mile back to my house. I held the back legs to keep the critter from clawing Elden, but every time Elden took a step, the jaws of the raccoon would open as Elden's right leg came close to its head. (The critter probably weighed a good twenty pounds.) I told Elden he was about to get bit.

So, Elden shifted the raccoon to his left leg and the raccoon got him in the left thigh instead of the right one. We were all a bloody mess by the time we got back to my house. There was an old 1936 Ford parked down by our barn. It had a trunk with a lid. (You can get a sense of how that worked by looking at the earlier photo of a 1936 Ford from the Tiller Mill stories.) So we put water and a carrot in the trunk of the car, dumped the raccoon in there and slammed the lid.

Mother disinfected the heck out of each wound and bandaged us all up. Elden and Jim left for home, and I checked on the raccoon before sunset. He had eaten the carrot and drunk the water. Raccoons are survivors. No question about it. Come morning, I got to feeling bad about that critter being held captive in the dark trunk, so I opened the lid, tossed in another carrot and left the lid open. He was gone the next time I checked, as was the carrot. For the next year, I'd occasionally see the track of a three-legged raccoon in the wet sand down along the river.

Little did I know until years later how worried our parents were that we might have been infected by a rabid critter. I guess all three families sweated it out for thirty days. And, no, none of us even got an infection in our wounds…thanks to Mom's soap and water, Mercurochrome, and band aids.

Violin Lessons

MOTHER WAS A LOVER OF music. She played the piano, had played the guitar for a while, and somewhere along the line she decided I needed to learn how to play the violin. She never explained that to me, and I never got around to asking why. Had I been given a choice, I'd have picked the guitar. But that came later.

For a year I sawed away on a new violin my parents bought me, traveled 22 miles once a week to Medford for violin lessons, learned how to read music and how to play the Blue Danube. ("Skaters away, skaters away…") I actually seemed to have some talent for the violin, but secretly I was mortified to admit I was playing such a sissy instrument.

To make matters worse, Benny was taking guitar lessons. At the end of the year, I talked mother into letting me stop taking violin lessons. And I never picked up a violin again. In a way, that was too bad.

Along about the eighth grade, a kid named Karl Weisbord sold me a battered guitar for five dollars so he would have someone to play guitar with, and that started me down the path of learning three chords and lick on the guitar. (And that's about all I play these days.)

The Jeep

I THINK I WOULD BE remiss if I didn't tell you about the surplus Army Jeep Dad drove home when I was about ten or so. It was a quarter ton four-wheel drive vehicle with an underpowered four-cylinder engine. I'm pretty sure Dad bought it to use as a work vehicle when he was still logging.

At any rate, I learned to drive thanks to the jeep. Dad would take it to the pasture we owned, the one Dean and Idelle later bought and filled with houses, stick it in 4WD, low range, tell me to not take it out of first gear and go ahead and drive it. I remember Cousin Terry being at our place a time or two, so we took turns. The jeep was so slow you could walk and keep up.

Eventually Dad told us to take the jeep down to a sandy place by the river and see if we could get it stuck. (But no side-hilling.) We'd get stuck and walk back to the house proud as punch. Dad would come down, look it over, say something like "good job," and then rock the little jeep out of the sand and tell us to try it again. We had a lot of fun, and I think I got to be a pretty good driver. I loved that jeep, and as we got older Dad let us drive it upriver on the old Bureau of Land Management roads and explore the country in and around Bear Mountain.

Kids grew up learning to drive at an early age. At age fourteen, I drove the jeep from Shady Cove to the pine country west of Chemult with Dad and John Dickinson as passengers. We were headed to camp and hunt deer. Now I'll admit to being a bit scared, but I would never have admitted it then.

Freedom is the only word for those times, and freedom was a key part of my growing up years. I know Mom worried about my exploration of the hills sometimes, but Dad would tell her I was a level-headed boy and it would be all right.

One more tale and then I'll move on. At my request, Dad took me upriver to a place just in below the Trail Rapids. (That's still visible from the highway just before you cross Trail Creek.) I had a big inner tube in the back of the jeep and I had my fly-fishing outfit.

I fished until nearly dark, put the tube in the water and floated home. My mother once said I had a Huck Finn childhood. If you add the trip in the old drift boat from Shady Cove to Dodge Bridge, I reckon she was right.

The old drift boat just got too old and leaky to use on the lakes anymore, so Dad parked it down by the river. I think he figured to give it kind of a Viking funeral and let the next flood float it away.

Jim, Elden and I got to eyeballing the boat and decided it was fixable, and if we patched the leaks with tar, it was good enough to float the river down to Dodge Bridge some few miles downriver…seven or eight miles, I'd guess. What we didn't figure on was the tar floating away from the cracks and messing with our fishing gear.

Loaded with some fishing tackle and fishing poles, and life jackets at Dad's insistence, we launched the boat right off a steep bank at the end of our pasture and into the river. We were pretty pleased with our repairs, but in below the Shady Cove bridge, we got sideways in the current and smacked a big rock hard enough to shoot a hammer right out of the boat and into the river.

That collision cracked the side of the boat, and sure enough it started leaking. The tar floated off the inside and before you knew it we were bailing water, and our poles, shoes and darned near everything else were coated with tar. We beached the boat around the first big bend below the Shady Cove bridge and took the poles to Elden's brother's place. But we were determined to continue on downriver to Dodge Bridge.

When Dodge Bridge was in sight, we were all in the water, holding onto the wooden boat, which insisted on floating, sort of, even though it was full of water and globs of floating tar. We did tie it to the back of Elden's pickup, took it home and put it back on the riverbank, and it did drift away on the next flood. If there is a moral to this story it might run along the lines of "If you patch a boat with tar, put it on the outside of the boat."

Other Classmates

There were girls in our class, of course, and on one level we were friends, but all through grade school they were more like sisters than girlfriends. That would change over time. Benny would marry Suzie Chubb. Jim would marry Linda Eccleston. The Swanson sisters, Glenda and Gloria would continue to snub us Shady Cove boys even though I secretly think Glenda liked me.

Once along about the sixth grade, Judy Mason, Linda Eccleston, Joan Huston and Suzie Chubb decided we boys should learn to dance. So they held a dance at Judy's house, chaperoned of course, and taught us a basic two-step routine. My dancing is still limited to a fundamental "stand and bounce in rhythm to the music."

The girls, especially Linda Eccleston, were for the most part better students than the rest of us. There was just too much sitting involved in the business of classroom instruction.

I won't bore my children and grandchildren with more details, although I might drum up a more detailed description of my classmates through my first ten years of school. Maybe.

High School

After Agness Brown was through with us, saw us tutored to pass the State of Oregon's Eighth Grade Examination (which included naming all the counties of the state and knowing Oregon became a state in 1859) and held an Eighth-Grade graduation ceremony in the small Apostolic Church, we were deemed ready to take the eleven-mile ride bus ride to Eagle Point High School.

My memory is a little shaky about the exact number of students at Eagle Point High School, but I think we numbered about 225 students, a congregation of Elk Creek Grade School, Shady Cove Grade School and Eagle Point Grade School. (At one time I think there was a Brownsville Grade School as well.) My old friend Dale Casey thinks there might have been about sixty freshmen, so the number comes close, and I'll leave it at that.

It wasn't a big school by any stretch, but we did have the largest high school gym in the state thanks to the donation of a huge gym by the Army when the Camp White base closed shop at the end of WWII. We could play three games on standard size basketball courts at the same time, and have a play on the stage while that was going on. It was long enough to make an echo.

I learned early we Shady Cove kids had a reputation of being a pretty rough crowd, and outlaws to boot. But our Shady Cove class turned out to be a pretty good bunch of students, and once again we had a crew of pretty darned good teachers.

Miss Olson was my freshman English teacher. She remembered my Uncle Dean from ten years earlier, not that she cut me any slack. But Agness Brown had me pretty well prepared in spelling and grammar, and I always had a yen to be a writer.

Our math teacher was also the coach, and the star football players set up front. He was determined to make sure his stars kept their grades up so they could play. In one six-week term, the coach did not call on me or mention my name. Enough said about that. I can still get pissed off if I thought about it for very long.

But I did well in algebra, and Pythagorean theorems in geometry made good sense in spite of some pretty poor teaching.

Basic science was taught by Mister Hay, a really great teacher. We were entertained and had a lot of fun. I can still remember him asking if experience was the best teacher. Of course, we all said yes. And then he gave us some examples to show some experiences might actually get us killed. Coming from a logging and mill town that lost at least a couple of men a year, we got it.

He also asked if reading in dim light was hard on our eyes. We all said yes. He then asked if total darkness was hard on our eyes. And so it went for the entire year. Nothing was taken for granted. He challenged us to think, but the challenge always came with a smile.

In our sophomore year, Mister Davies taught us Latin. I worked hard at it, as did my friend Dale. We thought we were pretty smart and pretty good at that Latin conjugation business, but I have to tell you I don't remember much beyond "*Britannia est insula*." (Britain is an island.) I do remember how dignified and proper Mister Davies was. A true scholar and a gentleman. He could have come straight out of an English school.

I was a fairly serious and a somewhat religious person in those days, and somehow I impressed some of our upper classmates, so they ran me for the office of Vice President of the student body. I had to make a speech, which was a bit scary, but I guess I did okay because I won the election. The speech ran along the line of, "I stand before you today to be judged, to be judged as your student body vice president.") I used that line one other time as a junior at Central High School. It worked the second time, too, and I was elected student body president.

I loved sports, anything that was an excuse to be in motion. The only thing I was very good at was track. As a freshman, I became the second fastest 100-yard low hurdle runner in our school, and I managed to earn a letter in my sophomore year.

Young Mister Braun was our biology teacher in our sophomore year. He was terrific. One of his lessons was basically about learning to observe and see what was going on about us. He took us to the football field and showed us how to catch snakes in the grass by the football field. Shoot, no one even knew any snakes were there. We were amazed and I took the lesson to heart. Kenny Williams and I became the chief snake catchers. The lesson was learned: look closely. There is probably a lot more going on in the natural world than you see at first glance. (Did you know snakes stink?)

And, of course, he taught us about photosynthesis. (I can still spell that correctly.) It's too bad our global warming experts missed that lesson. They would know CO_2 is absolutely key to our existence…and is not a toxic gas. It's plant food. Unless you run out of plants to process it back into O_2.

In shop class most of us learned drafting. I always got a B because my corners didn't perfectly line up. We also built cedar spice cabinets for our mothers. While we were doing basic stuff, our friend Jim Vanderlip was building a ski boat. (Jim always had more talent than he let on.)

First Real Job

1955 WAS THE SUMMER OF my 14th year, and I spent it working for Wally Crank in the Shady Cove Market. I was paid eighty-five cents an hour. At the end of the summer I had earned $596.00. At first I stocked shelves and carried groceries out to waiting cars. I think the title of my job was "box boy."

But as I learned more about the business, I moved up a bit and became sort of the "green grocer." I unpacked the veggie cases and "stocked" the veggie shelves. Wally would say, "Move the older stuff to the front and put the fresh stuff at the back." That's why I still always reach for the back of the veggies when I'm shopping.

My job didn't have the status of bucking hay bails on Ginger Roger's ranch, a choice job for some of my friends, located a few miles downriver from Shady Cove, but come Christmas I bought Dad a new .308 lever action rifle, Mom an electric skillet, and Gloria a Brownie Camera. I was pretty proud of myself.

Note: Dad was deer hunting with an old .32 Winchester Special and complained about missing a deer when the slug didn't penetrate the brush. So, by gollies, I fixed that. I still own the old .32. It joined the family in 1945, and I shot my first nine deer with it. After Dad died, I made sure Matthew, sister Debbie's son got the .308.

Religion

I WAS ALWAYS DRAWN TO churches and religion. Mom and Dad weren't much for going to church, but Grandma Opal and Grandpa Truman made sure I saw the inside of a church now and again. I liked the Reese Creek Church, a non-denominational affair. I learned to sing songs like "Rock of Ages," "Bringing in the Sheaves," "The Old Rugged Cross," and a lot of the other songs popular in the churches of old. But when they started taking me to the Apostolic Faith churches, my interest waned. Those people talked in tongues, and it scared the crap out of me.

That said, when Carol Scott invited me to church at the Trail Creek church, I decided to give it another try. I lasted as long a Carol rode the bus with me from Eagle Point High School, but when she got me "saved," she took up with another fellow and worked on him to get saved. (See my blog, "Vamping for Jesus.")

I stuck it out for a while. After all, I was a born-again Christian even if Carol moved on to fresh meat, but when the old ranter-preacher talked about sin and how even our thoughts could be sinful, and how it was a sin to covet a neighbor's wife or have sexual thoughts, I decided I had struck out. As an adolescent boy I had "thoughts." And since I was going to hell without a damned thing I could do about it, I quit the church, and it would be years and years later before I entered one for anything more than a wedding or a funeral.

Heart Attack

During my sophomore year, Dad was rushed to the hospital in Medford and diagnosed with a heart attack. I think he was about forty years old at the time. Our lives were suddenly and forever altered in ways that would take us from Shady Cove and the Rogue River, and from our friends.

Doc Beyers told Dad he would have to quit the woods and find a little easier occupation. I remember thinking I'd have to quit school and find a job to help support the family, but Dad insisted I go to school.

Sister Deborah

In the midst of this major disruption to our lives, I celebrated my fifteenth birthday on June 5, 1956, and Mother gave birth to a healthy baby girl on June 10. I don't know how Deborah's name was picked, but I think it was Mom's choice. (That's one of those questions that will go unanswered unless Deb can fill in that blank.) I remember thinking it was a blessing in the midst of our family disaster. She was more like a daughter to me than a sister, something that would change over time as we became adult friends.

Uncle Bill Walsh

I remember one trip to Diamond Lake during the summer Debbie was born. Uncle Bill Walsh was along. We had a campfire and I listened to the men talk. When Uncle Bill offered to help us our with our expenses, my heart was eased. I did not want to quit school. And I was forever grateful to Uncle Bill. Years later I wrote him a thank you letter and told him how much his offer meant to me.

I think Dad was grateful, too. But he had another idea for a business from which to make a living. He, Uncle Charles Hazelton, and Uncle Cliff Troop, with a small investment from John Dickinson as a silent partner, started an insurance brokerage in Medford. Before six months, they had thirteen insurance agents working for them, and a much bigger insurance brokerage in Los Angeles talking to them with an eye to buying them out. The number I heard Dad and my uncles use was a million dollar buy out. A million was a lot of money at that time.

I thought long and hard about not including the next part, but decided it was important to the story. Uncle Cliff was a con man and an alcoholic, a charming con man, a great storyteller, and fun to be with…for a few hours at a time. But, in the vernacular of the time, he went on a binge, cleaned out the brokerage account, and lost it all gambling in Reno.

Dad and Uncle Charles were threatened with jail time, but somehow scraped together enough money to pay off the money owed to the insurance companies. It broke the business. Dad talked John Dickinson out of having Cliff arrested. Over the years, Cliff milked Mom and Dad for help numerous times. I once asked Dad why he put up with that sonofabitch, and he said, "Because he's your mother's brother." End of story.

So, Dad had to find a job, and Carl Scott, a logger who lived near the little town of Trail put him to running his little power saw shop in Shady Cove. It suited Dad, and we had an income again.

After a few months, I remember Dad coming home from the power saw shop. He looked pretty grim. He told Mom the shop was losing money, and Carl Scott didn't know it, but he was honor bound to tell Carl and show him the books.

Carl was grateful, but he closed the shop shortly thereafter. And we were stuck. Most of our savings were gone, Dad couldn't do any of the heavy work tied to logging, and jobs were scarce in the wintertime anyway. The jeep had been sold to raise money for the brokerage, Dad's pickup was also sold, along with his power saws, chokers, etc.

That was when Bob Frost called and asked Dad if he would come to Independence, Oregon, and run his wrecking yard, Andy's Auto Wreckers. The plan was for Dad to run the business while Bob looked for and bought salvage vehicles.

Mom and Dad talked it over and said they would move at the end of the school year, but not before. Bob said that would be okay.

In late spring, Mom and Dad sold the place to Grandma Opal Collins. Grandpa had died from a heart attack some years earlier. I think I was about thirteen when he died. We packed up our goods and Mom and Dad, Gloria, Debbie and I moved to Independence.

In some ways, it turned out to be a good move for me. I turned sixteen, got my driver's license, and Bob gave me a job in the wrecking yard working for my dad. (And Dad and I managed to stay friends.)

It was a long, lonesome summer. I missed my friends and the river and our family in Southern Oregon. But I learned to use a cutting torch, drive the wrecker to pick up wrecked cars and to deliver car parts, and do basic mechanical work. And piece by piece, with Dad's help, I built a good 1950 2-door Ford sedan with a 1953 Mercury flathead engine with a 4-barrel carb. And when a wreck came in with top-of-the-line nylon Double Eagle tires, I bought them for my car.

Baby Sister Debbie, almost 3, in front of my "new" 1950 Ford

Basically, I just wrote my work hours on the calendar and drew very little money from that base. When school started, I had new clothes, a freshly painted car in Robin's Egg Blue, and a flat top haircut. I was ready for a new adventure.

First Day At Central

I DROVE MY FORD TO Central High School which was located in the two-mile stretch of road between Independence and Monmouth, Oregon, parked my car (nobody locked cars in those days), took a deep breath and walked to the front door. A tall kid was staring at me, and when I mounted the steps he stuck out his hand and said, "You're new aren't you? I'm Tom Hill. Let me show you around."

I'll forever be grateful to Tom. He made my transition a whole lot easier than it might have. He took me to see Coach Heater, and I got signed up for football, and he took me around and introduced me to some of my soon-to-be classmates.

During the first week of football practice, I took my 145 pounds of dynamite into the fray. The coach was running what he called "man or mouse" drills, a training drill in blocking other players. I dumped one kid on his back. I thought, "Huh, oh," but he bounced back up and said, "Who did that?"

Primed to throw the first punch, I said, "I did." He stuck out his hand and said, "Coach, we got us a new player." And that's how I met Aaron Cooper who is still a close friend after all these years. He managed to dump me on my back during the next 'man or mouse' drill.

There is a story I like to tell about how Aaron and I cemented our friendship. The teacher for our speech class was late getting to the room, so Coop stood up and said, "I don't suppose any of you sonsabitches can get up at four and go duck hunting."

I waited about five seconds, and when no one responded, I said, "I can." We hunted ducks together for rest of the season and became lifelong friends. Coop wasn't very big, but he was tougher than hell.

Off the football field, I was only challenged physically once. A cute girl in my class named Betty Crane told me there was always a Friday night dance after a home game. I asked her if I could take her to the dance. She told me, a lie I was late in figuring out, you go to the dance and then take a girl home. So, being brand new there, I went to the dance and gave her a ride home afterwards.

The next Monday, as I was walking down the hallway minding my own business, a kid about my size bumped into me, hard. I moved over and he did too and bumped me again. I asked him what his beef was and he clobbered me. But I was trained by Dean Collins and the bullies in Shady Cove Grade School, so I hit him with a hard left to his solar plexus, and when he bent over, I hit him with a right upper cut. I missed his nose, but I did hit him in the forehead hard enough to raise a knot.

Dewey Cummins, who later became a good friend, broke up the fight and pushed us into the bathroom before any of the teachers got there. I asked the kid who hit me, "What's was going on? I don't even know your name."

He said, "I was just finding out how tough you are."

And that's the story of how I whipped the toughest kid in school, Walt Samadorf. He was still the toughest kid in school, but nobody messed with me ever again. I was to learn later that Dick Britton, who was a whole lot bigger than I was, sicced Walt on me because he was sweet on Betty. I didn't date Betty for very long. She told me she was just trying to make Dick Jealous. Dick died a few years ago, in 2019 I think it was…but we were never friends. And he and Betty never married.

Coop and I hunted ducks through the season, got chased out of the Eola Wildlife Reservation by a game warden named Scriptner (I have no idea if that's the right spelling, but that's how it sounded), but he couldn't catch my Ford. And we went on hunting, and we kept hand loading more and more powerful shotgun shells until one peeled the barrel of Aaron's model 12-gauge shotgun.

I was a pretty solemn, serious boy at Eagle Point High School, a role assigned me by the kids I grew up with, and it wasn't a role I liked very much. So, I sort of reinvented myself at Central High School. I was social, outgoing, and friendly. And I liked that style a whole lot better than being super serious all the time.

Coop and Lynn Wilson, both of whom were seniors, didn't like the kid who was running for Student Body President, so they ran me. And danged if I didn't win. I didn't take the business of campaigning very seriously, so in my speech to the students at the assembly to introduce the candidates, I promised a day out of school. And I won the election.

Later I talked the principal into having a clean-up day around the school and in the local fields and along the highway and I delivered on my promise. Good thing I never liked politics, I reckon. I was good at it. Might have ruined my life.

The summer following my junior year, I was hired by Gene Clark, a local farmer to work in his grain cleaner, but there was about a three-week delay while the rye grass headed out. So I took Gloria to the strawberry fields and we picked strawberries for a couple of weeks, and it rained, and we came home with mud all over us. I think Gloria earned about four dollars a day

The Collins family story of resilience, kindness. strength, and laughter

in the berries, and I earned about eight dollars…which was okay money at the time. Gas was about nineteen cents a gallon. Depending on the gas wars among service stations, it was sometimes 16 or 17 cents a gallon.

That was the only time Gloria and I ever worked together, but I remember those few days fondly. She was proud and I was proud of her.

After a very short strawberry season, I filled in the time picking cherries. I earned about twelve dollars a day. I liked propping a ladder in a tree and starting at the top, picking my way down. I was what I would call a "second tier" picker, faster than the slowest, but slower than the best, some of whom could pick thirty boxes a day compared to my twelve.

Cherry picking only lasted a few days, and then the rye grass harvest started and it was off to the grain cleaner for the rest of the summer. My job ran from 11:00 p.m. until 8:00 a.m. I weighed sacks and made sure there was an even one-hundred pounds of rye seed in each sack. Then I sewed each sack with a sack needle and heavy twine, stacked it on a hand truck, and when I had five sacks, I'd run the load to the back of the barn and hurry back in time to tip the deflector and start filling a new sack. It was always a close call. The grain cleaner was just across our driveway, through a gate and into the barn where the grain cleaner was set up.

After lifting one-hundred-pound sacks all summer, I was in pretty darned good shape come football season.

I also sampled the grain, and if I found too much foreign seed or woody material in the rye, I'd shut the shaker off and clean the screens. It didn't happen too often, but it took time.

Three things I think are important about that time: First, the grain cleaner was so loud the radio with the volume turned all the way up could not be heard over the noise of the motor; Second, when I took my lunch break along about 4:00 a.m., the quiet was wonderful and the night sky was brilliant with stars…and you could see Orion; Third, I had this great block of time after a shower and a sleep. I could play a round of golf, take my girlfriend to a movie, and still get back in time for work.

On one early afternoon, I think it was a Saturday, I drove to Tom Hill's house in Independence to visit. We got to talking and I discovered he had never been to the beach, and his greatest adventures included a school trip to Mount Hood, a quick drive across the Columbia River to Vancouver, Washington and back, and south to Corvallis, a great galloping twenty miles away.

I told him to get in the car. He wanted to know where we were going. I said, "The beach." It was only sixty miles to Neskowin where Dad and I surf-fished for yellow fin a time or two. Tom waded in the surf and then flopped down and rolled in the water like a puppy dog. By gollies, he was seventeen when he saw the ocean for the first time.

To cap off this story, Tom and I were freshman at Oregon College of Education. On one sunny spring day, we were walking down the sidewalk on the main street through the campus, and as we approached the admin building, Tom said right out of blue, "I have never been anyplace." He walked into the admin building and withdrew from school, introduced Dave Richardson to Sue (who is still married to Dave some sixty plus years later), took Dave to the grocery store in Independence and introduced him as Tom's replacement. And he gave me a fifth of whisky he had never opened. (Tom wasn't a drinker and it made me wonder why he had the whisky in the first place.)

And then he enlisted in the Air Force and spent his whole Air Force career in San Antonio, Texas. He still lives there with his wife of many years, surrounded by his children and grandchildren. And I'm still not sure he ever made it to anyplace other than San Antonio or back to Independence from time to time.

During my senior year of high school I got acquainted with some professors at the local college. When I say local, I mean it. Central High School and the Oregon College of Education were only about one mile apart. I had written a senior paper about the "Wall" in Berlin, Germany and why I thought it was a major issue for my generation. Mister Matzio, my English teacher, fed the article to a friend at the college, and darned if I wasn't invited to present the paper at a faculty luncheon.

It was a little intimidating, but I really thought I had done a good analysis so I sucked it up and plowed ahead. After I read my paper, and answered a few gentle questions, I got a mild round of applause from the twenty or so professors, and ate a nice lunch.

It must have been an okay presentation because later I received a scholarship to the college that I hadn't applied for. I think it helped seal my decision to attend school there.

Farmhouse

WE LIVED IN A BIG two-story farmhouse on a road that ran between old Highway 99 and Independence, sort of a back road. It had five bedrooms upstairs and a master bedroom and an old-fashioned parlor downstairs that could be used as a bedroom in a pinch. So, realistically, it was a seven-bedroom house with a full basement and a huge walk-in pantry. And one bathroom.

Somehow, and I don't remember the details, Juanita and Charles Hazelton wound up with serious financial problems, so my folks offered them shelter until they got back on their feet. For six months during my senior year, Leah, Linda, Uncle Charles and Aunt Juanita lived with us. And I think they felt both gratitude and resentment. It was very hard on them. The word "depression" has dropped out of use to describe financial conditions, so I'll just say there was a "recession" in Oregon at the time and a lot of people were temporarily out of work.

Uncle Charles was a licensed landscape architect, and he finally found a job with Oregon Department of Transportation in Portland, Oregon. Freeways were a new business in Oregon, and those in power wanted our freeways to look nice, so tree planting, irrigation systems and landscaping were in vogue. It fit his skills nicely.

By the time Juanita and Charles moved on up to Portland, we were darned near broke again. My folks didn't begrudge the help they gave, but I think this was about when I decided life isn't fair.

Baby sister Debbie and I pose for a graduation photo

High school graduation was one of the happiest days of my life. I was more than ready to leave public schools and move on to what I believed was the more rarefied air of college life.

I had a better guitar by then, better than the one Karl Weisbroad had found for me. Late in my senior year of high school, there was a talent contest, and Bob Marr and Cal Wisenflue and I worked all of ten minutes in the hallway learning all the words to Thunder Road, a three-chord lick and bit of harmony, and then trotted out in the gym and sang. By gollies we won the talent contest. Bob had a good voice, and I could harmonize. I can't for the life of me remember if Cal could sing or not. That led later in my college days to singing in a quartet with Bob, John Fisher and Gary. His last name will come to me, I'm sure. But I'll save that story for later.

Starting Over…Again

A WORD ABOUT THE MOVE to Caldwell, Idaho. Dad quit Andy's Wrecking after a run-in with Bob's silent partner, an attorney from Salem. The guy walked into the shop, drunk and abusive, and Dad took it. I was there, so I speak from first-hand knowledge. On the way back to the house after we closed up, he was fuming. When he said, "Before the heart attack, I would not have taken that."

I asked, "Then why take it now?"

Dad did a U-turn, and we went back to the wrecking yard and packed up all of Dad's tools. When we got home, he called Bob's partner and told him where to stick it. I think that was the point in time when my dad recovered from the worry about the heart attack and went back to living without nagging fear. (I quit my part-time job there at the same time.)

Bob Frost told his attorney partner that he shouldn't have run Dad off, and then told him to buy Bob out. Which the attorney did.

In those days, you could buy a dealer's license in Idaho for one-hundred dollars, providing you had an office, a sign, a desk, a phone and a filing cabinet. In Oregon you had to have a $10,000 bond. There were also other restrictions to deal with in Oregon that weren't found in Idaho. (Which might explain why Idaho at that time was a haven for stolen cars.)

Dad and Bob spent the next few months horse trading, buying and selling vehicles and putting together an inventory of used pickups, one jeep, an old

Ford "Woody" station wagon, and a couple of trucks. Dad refused to move until I graduated.

So, along about the third week of May, 1959, I helped them load all their belongings into one of the big trucks, waved goodbye to my sisters and my folks, cleaned the house and gave the key to Gene Clark, the farmer who owned the place...and for whom I had worked at the grain cleaner.

Waving goodbye as my family moved to Caldwell, Idaho

Before starting my summer job with the highway department in Portland, a job Uncle Charles got me, I spent a few days working for the Cummins brothers. They had contracts with a number of farmers to shear sheep. The brothers were sheep shearing champions, a title won by Dewey, the oldest brother at the State Fair, and won the next year by Harry, brother number two, the next year. Along with little brother Dwight, they sheared up to three hundred sheep a day.

At the rate of one dollar per sheep, it added up to big money in those days.

My job was to grab a sheep by the jaw, dump it on it's butt and slide it to whoever needed another sheep. In between times, I stuffed a long cotton sack hanging from the rafters with wool, and packed it by dropping down from above the sack and tamping it down. By the end of the day, my jeans were so coated with lanolin I could darned near stand them in a corner. I can't remember what the brothers paid, but it was enough, and they gave me a bedroom and meals.

And then it was off to Portland. Uncle Charles took me to the Department of Motor Vehicles to get my chauffeur's license because it meant an extra forty dollars a month from the highway department if I had one. And as it turned out, I drove a truck most of the summer. It was a lot better than pulling weeds.

I don't know how Leah and Linda felt about sharing a house with me, but Uncle Charles told me I was welcome and said it was a way of paying my folks back for shelter at the big farmhouse. Life seemed a little fairer then.

On a Monday, I drove my Ford to 60th and Glisan and met my boss and about five other college kids, all young men, who were my workmates for the summer. Basically, we were paid to groom the landscaping along the new Banfield freeway headed east out of Portland. At that time, the freeway ended at Troutdale but the landscaping ended along about 182nd, assuming my memory is correct.

The first two weeks were spent pulling weeds and grooming the shrub beds, but because I had a chauffeur's license, by week three I was told to take the water truck which had a thousand-gallon tank and go water the new trees between the Willamette River and the 182nd exit or at least close to there.

As the summer dried the grass along the train tracks running parallel to the freeway, it wasn't uncommon for the sparks from the steel wheels on the trains to set the grass on fire. Then it was a race between me and my gravity drained water truck and the fire department. I'm happy to say, I beat them more than once. It made a good break from the monotony of taking care of water starved trees.

By the end of summer I had enough money in savings to see me through my first year. It did mean selling my beloved Ford, but I never gave it a second thought. I was free of car insurance, license fees, the cost of gasoline, tires and the whole business of keeping a car running. Uncle Dean had cautioned me about not becoming the campus chauffeur, and he proved right. The people who did have cars were constantly pestered for rides.

I did make one new friend that summer, Michael Engel. He had a Vespa motor scooter, and we spent some weekends tooting around Portland, watching "Bell, Book and Candle" at the Blue Mouse theater downtown, hunting up bakeries for good French bread and playing chess. He was a better player, but I won a game now and then. I'm still suspicious he allowed that because he won the Oregon State University chess tournament the year before. The whole block where the Blue Mouse sat was demolished and replace by taller buildings a few years later.

A word about the Vespa scooter of those days. On a steep hill, the passenger had to get off and push. I will say I was convinced to never own one.

The Hazeltons left on vacation for two weeks that summer, so I batched. My first move was to go buy a box mix of spice cake, mix up the batter and eat it. Finally, I actually had enough raw batter to myself. I did not have to lick the bowl. I ate it.

The house was on 80th and Division, not far from Mount Tabor, and on some evenings I'd hike to the top of Mount Tabor and take in the view as the sun set. And on the weekends, I rode the Rose City bus. I bought a map of the city, and set out to learn where everything was. I'd get on the bus at 82nd and Division, one headed in the direction of downtown, ride to the end of the line, get a transfer and ride a new route to the end of the line, and transfer again or ride back to a main line. I think I had a pretty clear picture of the city by the end of summer. That was before I-405, I-5, and I-205 interfered with the regular streets. Those freeways turned my picture of Portland into a knot of streets I have a tough time unraveling these days.

Caldwell

While I was busy working in Portland for the summer, Dad and Bob were busy building up a used truck business in Caldwell, Idaho, and making a go of it. They had a contact in Cedar Rapids, Iowa who worked in the International Harvester store. His name was Howdy. I never heard a last name.

Vehicles traded in for newer ones at Howdy's store were either held or sold, and those that didn't sell within ninety day were wholesaled to other truck dealers. When Howdy had three trucks ready for wholesale, he'd call and Bob would fly back, put a piggyback hook up together and drive the trucks back to Bob and John's truck shop in Idaho.

Dad and Bob bought a rundown place along Highway 30 between Caldwell and Nampa, remodeled a chicken shed into an office, made a deck out of planks for mechanical work, and put up a sign. They were in business.

Later in life they would own sixteen acres along Highway 30 between Caldwell and Nampa, a big shop that employed twelve mechanics, a parts store, a body and fender shop, and a wrecking yard.

After coming close to building himself an ulcer and trying to convince Bob the dealership was losing money on a regular basis, Dad sold out to Bob and a silent partner and just worked for them selling trucks. One year Dad was International Harvester's salesman of the year. That was worth a new .308 rifle, camping gear and tickets to Hawaii. Much to Mother's displeasure the tickets were raffled off to the people working for the company. A recently married young woman drew the tickets. I'm convinced Dad rigged it. And I'm convinced Mother remained a bit irritated with Dad for quite a while. He said he'd had enough travel thanks to the Army. Mother had not.

Jarvis Jeep

But back to my final days with the Hazelton's in Portland. Jarvis Jeep had a running ad for a jeep. They always had one for sale for three hundred dollars. So I thought about it, talked to Dad on the phone and asked if that was too much money to pay for a jeep. When I told Dad I was thinking I could buy one, drive it to Caldwell and he could put it on his used truck lot, he said, "If it is in good shape, I can probably get you around five hundred for it."

So off to Jarvis Jeep I went. The salesman I talked to kept showing me jeeps that were a lot more than three hundred dollars. I finally got fed up and said, "You don't really have a Jeep for three hundred dollars. This is just a switch pitch."

He took me back into the yard where vehicles were stored and showed me a nice-looking Jeep pickup…for three hundred dollars. I drove it, checked the oil, looked the tires over, inspected the drive train for leaks, looked the engine over for leaks as well, and paid three hundred dollars for it.

I paid for a temporary vehicle license, stowed my personal gear in it, which wasn't much in those days, and nursed the Jeep on to Caldwell at about fifty miles an hour so I could brag about what good mileage it got.

The Collins family story of resilience, kindness. strength, and laughter

When I finally found Mom and Dad's house in Caldwell, Mom, Gloria, and Debbie all came running out the front door. I'm not ashamed to admit I cried a bit. Except for that stint in Long Beach, I had never been away so long.

I think two emotions were at work. First, I was sad about the circumstances that led them to move away from home, again. Second, I didn't know how lonesome I had been for my family. Mother cried a little with me that time. I guess she missed me, too.

That deal with the Jeep made me an extra two hundred dollars for college, but it wasn't a straight deal. Unbeknownst to me, the front differential on the Jeep was missing an axle. Which meant it really wasn't a 4-wheel drive after all. Dad had swapped the Jeep for a Chevy pickup and $300, so any profit was in the Chevy. I'd have to wait until the Chevy pickup sold.

After I left for school, Dad told me the guy who bought the Jeep had stormed back in and told him about getting stuck up in the hills because the 4-wheel drive wouldn't work. That's when Dad told him about the bent tie-rods and the busted shock absorber on the Chevy the man had failed to mention. They finally agreed it was an even-up deal. Dad replaced the tie-rods on the Chevy pickup, and shocks were cheap in those days, so when it was fixed, he sold it for two hundred fifty dollars and sent me the money. (Fifty dollars covered the cost of parts to repair the thing.)

I know this much, that venture didn't encourage me to get into the used vehicle business. I also took a certain grim pleasure when Jarvis Jeep went out of business. You can't lie to people and not expect it to bite you.

To School

One of the guys I worked the summer with was headed for Willamette University in Salem, so after I rode Greyhound back to Portland from Caldwell, he picked me up and dropped me off in Monmouth. His name will come to me, I'm sure.

So there I was, in Monmouth, standing in front of Maaske Hall, the dorm that would be my new home for the next few months, wondering where in the heck I was supposed to go. I walked into the dorm, found a guy sitting at a table, told him who I was and asked him where I was supposed to go. He gave me a Freshman Beanie, told me I had to wear it at all times on campus, and told me to take my gear to the basement because of some mix-up about housing, and told me to choose a cot. (I did not wear the beanie.)

That led to making friends with Dave Richardson. I dumped my gear on a cot and a voice from somewhere in the corner said, "You can't have that. It's reserved for the football players." I was irritated by whole affair. I paid for a room, and all I was getting was a cot in the basement?

I said, "This is my cot. Any football player can choose his own cot, but not this one." A voice from the cot next to mine said, "They can't have mine either." It was Dave, and we have been friends ever since.

We spent two nights on the cots and were finally assigned rooms on the third floor of Maaskey Hall. Dave drew Kent Smith for a roommate and I drew a nice kid named Dave McMurray. Dave Richardson and I talked about making a trade so we could room together, but finally voted against it. So Dave McMurray and I were roommates for one school year and classmates for the following three. In my memory Dave McMurray remains one of the most decent people I ever met. And Kent turned out to be a mooch.

I'll make this part brief. I will confess to majoring in beer that first year, but I did pull Bs in all of my classes.

All incoming freshmen were given a written test. Based on the test a select few were placed in the Honors Program. I was one of the lucky few. We had access to the best teachers, and the curriculum was a notch above the standard survey classes most freshmen endure. The survey classes were basically a review of what we studied in high school. I was glad to miss most of those.

Dorm life paled along about Spring quarter, so Dave and I rented a small apartment off campus ($35 a month) for which we were called into the Dean's office. Freshmen were required to live in the dorm unless they commuted from home. We won the Dean, Doctor Glogau, over with our serious demeanor and our assertions it was impossible to study in the dorm, and we had already paid for our dorm rooms anyway, and we were still eating in the cafeteria. To this day, I don't know if he was concerned about our safety or about our money. I'd bet on the money if I had to choose.

The Lamron

THE SCHOOL WAS OPERATING A Big Brother/Big Sister program. My Big Brother was a guy named Fred Staab, and through him I got acquainted with another upperclassman, Ralph Wirfs. At 6'7" Ralph was the tallest person

I had ever met, but I wasn't much intimidated. Along about Spring quarter, Fred and Ralph cornered me in the Student Union where coffee was still a nickel a cup. They told me they wanted me to apply for the job of editor of the college newspaper the *Lamron*. (Oregon College of Education had earlier in its history been a "normal" school for training teachers. It's pretty obvious how the newspaper got its name.)

I wasn't interested because I could see both of them wanted to be the shadow power behind the editor. But when they told me the job paid tuition and fees, I got a lot more interested. So I took my eighteen years of life experience, attended a student body meeting, and applied. I had to give a little speech, but I told the council I had written a novel, which I had, just to amuse myself during my senior year of high school. I guess some members of the student council were impressed, and I was chosen over the more experienced assistant editor, a nice young woman I talked into staying on. Shoot, I had no idea how the newspaper was put together, and she did. I look back and I think how unfair it was to choose me over her. Yep...and life was again not fair.

So, in my sophomore year, I was the editor of the *Lamron*. About forty students volunteered to help, and I was faced with my first "reduction in force." There simply wasn't enough work for that many people on a four-page once-a-week rag. I finally, and sadly, pruned the staff down to sixteen people, held a meeting and said my goals were simple: always tell the truth, put out a paper students and faculty would want to read, write straight news stories, always meet our deadlines, print an error-free newspaper, and make it the best small college newspaper in the country. We did win a minor award later in the year. The name of the award escapes me.

And while I listened to Fred and Ralph, I went my own way. I'm sure they were disappointed. More importantly, I listened to my assistant editor. She gave me her complete support. I still don't know why. But maybe Fred nailed it when he said, "I don't know how you do it, Rod, but you build *esprit de corps*." I intended to.

I never seemed to earn enough money from the summer work to carry me through an entire school year, so I worked as a school bus driver my sophomore year, along with my buddy Dave Richardson, edited the *Lamron*, and worked in the bookstore. There I became the paperback books manager for $1.25 an hour. But the hours were flexible, so it was manageable.

It may sound unbelievable in this day and age, but there were only two bookstores at that time in the Salem area, one at Willamette University, and one at OCE. This was before book racks in grocery stores. There were no other commercial bookstores. When I started working in the OCE bookstore, we carried about a thousand paperback titles, a pretty puny offering for a college. So whenever we received a publisher's catalog, I circulated it among the professors I trusted and asked which titles we should order. When those came in, I'd let the professors know and they would tell their students.

By the end of the year we carried about five thousand titles, and gross sales move from $90,000 a year to $270,00 dollars a year. And teachers from all around the area began shopping in our store.

I only got in trouble with the "real" manager, Otto when I started moving his inventory of logo sweatshirts, cups and other souvenirs to the back room to make room for "my" books. I don't think Otto ever understood what was going on.

I made several lifelong friends in my years on campus, I played the role of Scapin in an original stage play, I had the honor of escorting Basil Rathbone to a reception on campus, I met and married Maggie Hanna, and I celebrated a delayed graduation at the end of six years.

The delay was caused in part by an adventure to Alaska. At the end of my sophomore year, Benny Nork and I drove the ALCAN highway to Anchorage and spent most of the summer working and doing a little fishing. I also took a four-month trip to Mexico. Both trips meant an extra year or so in college.

And I missed my first junior year thanks to two bouts of pneumonia which encouraged the doctor to call my parents and tell them I wasn't going to survive a third bout, so why didn't they just come and get me and take me home. Which they did.

I healed up, worked three part-time jobs because I couldn't find one good one, and because I wanted to save enough money for another try at my second Junior year. About mid-Spring, Uncle Charles called and asked if I wanted to work for Solomon Aichele Landscaping. Uncle Charles was foreman on a landscaping job around the I-84 Ontario, Oregon, freeway exchange. He offered me three dollars an hour, more than double what my other jobs paid. It didn't take me long to say yes.

Dad and Bob Frost were doing well in the used truck business, and when Dad took a 1956 Ford sedan in trade, I bought it. The only thing wrong with it was a cut in the right rear fender that looked like someone had taken an axe and whacked it. I cleaned it up, used liquid metal putty, sanded it down and bought a small can of matching paint. When I was done, you couldn't tell it had ever been damaged.

That gave me transportation from Caldwell to Ontario each morning. I learned how to plant sumac trees, clean the pipes on the sprinkler system and pull weeds…again. I sometimes think even now that I'm cursed by weed pulling. It never ends.

Back to Portland

THE JOB MOVED FROM ONTARIO back to the Portland area, and I moved back in with Uncle Charles and Aunt Juanita for a time. We put in the plumbing and the sprinkler system at Multnomah Falls parking area and at the Lewis and Clark State Park where I-84 crosses the Sandy River. At the Dodson interchange upriver from Multnomah Falls, we moved rock and cleaned up the area alongside the "loop" off the freeway. I was still making $3.00 an hour, digging holes with a shovel and building fence while the other three young men on the crew were driving tractor and dump trucks at about $3.50 an hour.

When Solomon asked if anyone wanted to learn how to operate a backhoe, they all turned it down. I think I might have waited all of five second before saying, "I do." He told me I would still earn the labor wage while I was learning. I said I didn't care. (Anything was better than picking up rock and pounding fence posts into rocky ground.)

Solomon, a great guy and a war hero, fought across Europe in Patton's Third Army as a tank sergeant. And he continued to bark just like he had when in the army. But he liked the young men he hired and trusted them to get the job done, so we pretty much ignored the growls he sometimes threw our way.

The last job we did in the Portland area was the sprinkler system on the Mount Scott golf course. It was a big job and earned Solomon pretty good money. I was still operating the backhoe and digging trenches, but when it came to digging up the fairways, he brought in a smaller machine to dig trenches and put me in charge of digging the smaller lines. I don't think we did the whole golf course, just a nine-hole section.

Took us a month, and then it was off to Eugene to landscape the freeway from the Willamette River I-5 bridge and north for a distance of eighteen miles. Dave Richardson was working for the Oregon Department of Transportation in Eugene while Sue finished her master's degree in education at the University of Oregon.

They were renting a two-story apartment in West Eugene, and when Dave suggested I use their upstairs bedroom, I jumped at the chance. The rent was about sixty dollars a month, so I offered to pay the rent while I stayed there.

When Dave was assigned as the inspector for our landscaping job, he looked at the wage scale in the contract and found backhoe operators were to be paid $4.03 an hour. That made me the second highest paid member of the crew. There was some grumbling until Solomon laughed and reminded them they had their chance to learn how to operate a backhoe and turned it down. The highest paid operator was the cat skinner and I don't know how much he was paid. He was as tight-lipped about that as I was.

Sol paid us every Friday afternoon, and the guys would start comparing paychecks. When they asked me how much I made, I would offer to take their checks and pay their bills if they would do the same for me. And that was all I would say. I never told them because I didn't figure it was any of their business.

Part of the job called for planting trees around the Q Street interchange, but Solomon and Uncle Charles had not checked the ground to see if there was any soil to plant the trees in. So we wound up digging holes for each tree and using dump trucks to bring in top soil. Uncle Charles would set a stake, and I would dig a one-yard hole three feet by three feet by three feet. That would later be filled with topsoil for tree planting.

Once the holes were dug, it was time to drive dump truck, and I took about a forty-cent cut in pay, but I didn't mind. By this time we knew Sol and Uncle Charles were in trouble financially. The crew agreed to donate a couple of hours each day in order to keep Sol from going broke. We also donated a couple of Saturdays.

When I returned to college that fall, I had a good car, some decent clothes for a change, and enough money to just be a student for the first two terms, no jobs. I'll add this much, I knuckled down and became a serious student, and pulled pretty decent grades even if I did go back to work Spring quarter.

The Columbus Day Storm

ONE OF THE BIG EVENTS of that year was the Columbus Day storm. I was sharing a small house with Jerry Braaten when the storm rolled in unannounced. We lost power, and as we watched, the big fir trees in The Grove on campus near Campbell Hall started going down. When that happened, I knew we were in trouble. The storm came in from the south. The only thing we could do was move into the bedroom on the north side of the house, drop the blinds on all the windows to stop any broken glass if the windows gave way, close the doors and ride it out. Early on, we ducked next door to the Wagon Wheel Café and filled a thermos with coffee because their grill was gas powered and they had put on a big pot of coffee.

So, we nursed a hot cup of coffee, fired up a small Hibachi, cooked hot dogs, played cards, and just hunkered down to wait it out. The wind roared and shook the house. We later learned it was over one-hundred miles an hour. We could hear the limbs of a fruit tree on the south side of the house banging on the roof. Jerry ran out and drove the front end of his car on the root wad, but all that did was raise the front end of the car every time a strong gust hit the tree. I should say I was sorry, but the sight was enough to make me laugh.

It was dark before it all settled down. Come daylight the big fir trees in the grove were almost all down, and the steeple on Campbell Hall had toppled. We later heard one of the students who rode my school bus was killed by a falling tree. What he was doing out in the storm is anybody's guess.

A classmate snapped three pictures of the steeple on Campbell Hall showing the first tilt, the toppling of the steeple, and a photo of the steeple in midair. Those were published in Life Magazine and I'm told our classmate went on to be a well-known photographer. Unfortunately, I can't remember his name right now, but what the heck. That about sixty years ago.

First Marriage

FOR SOME REASON I HAVE a hard time understanding now, during my second junior year, I rekindled an earlier romance with Margaret Hanna, aka

"Maggie." The end result was two fine daughters, Jennifer, born February 18, 1968 and Catherine, born April 9 1969. I'll not comment about the quarrels and recriminations leading up to a divorce after eleven years of marriage. Let me put it this way: we quarreled the night before our big church wedding, and I'm sure if we each had the courage, we would have called it off. I look at Jennifer and Catherine, and I'm glad we didn't.

It wasn't all bad. I can look back on three summer seasons on a fire lookout in the North Warner Mountains of the Lakeview Ranger District, Fremont National Forest not too far north of Lakeview, Oregon. We spent one season on Abert Rim and two on Drake Peak. And I can look back on a five-month trek into Mexico. But on balance, the marriage was more misery than joy for me, and I suspect for her as well.

Graduation

I PROBABLY SCREWED AROUND TOO much with the trip up the ALCAN Highway through Canada to Alaska with Benny Nork, the trip to Mexico, and a lost year to pneumonia, but I finally graduated in 1965, just short of six years after I first enrolled at OCE.

My first teaching job was at North Marion High School in the little town of Hubbard a few miles north of Woodburn, Oregon. Maggie and I both had contracts to teach English. I didn't realize it would forever be the best teaching job I would ever have. I loved the classroom and my students, but I didn't get along well with some of the teachers. I'd find them gossiping about some young student, saying things like, "Well, what do you expect. I had her older brother in class and he was incorrigible. The whole family is like that."

At the end of the school year, I was offered a contract to teach another year at North Marion, but I turned it down. After nineteen years in school in one capacity or another, I decided I had better see what else was out there "in the real world."

I worked out the summer in the North Warner mountains on the Fremont National Forest, thinking my score of 100 on the forestry tech roster was going to get me a permanent job. My boss was Don Reynolds, and his wife told Maggie they were going to hire me in January. So, we moved to Lakeview, rented an apartment and waited. Two months later, make that along about the first of March, I finally woke up. There was no job offer coming, or if one did come it would be late May. Savings from summer work simply wouldn't last that long. And because I had taught school the year before, I wasn't eligible for unemployment insurance. Jobs were scarce in Lakeview in the winter, so it was time to pack up and head for Salem where we rented a decent apartment overlooking the River Road between Salem and Independence.

When I went back to the service station where I worked a full year, Maurice Dodson laughed and said, "You have a degree. You don't want to do this kind of work." I assured him I did indeed, but he wouldn't budge.

That started a chain of events that damned near took away all of my self-confidence. I would interview for a job each morning, and then go home and write. Maggie was working for the Valley Migrant League, so we were getting by, but after fifty interviews and no job offers, I was approaching despair. I had never spent more than a couple of hours finding a job. Not even in Alaska right in the middle of a strike. And now all I was hearing was "no."

I finally made a game of it. I thought of it as practicing the art of interviewing. I even took the test at Sears because I thought it would be fun to work in the sporting goods department. The personnel officer for the Salem store came out of her office and said, "None of our applicants ever scored this high." I perked up until she said, "You can do better than work for us. Besides, you would never stay."

And then one magic day, a friend who worked for the Oregon Department of Education called me and asked if I would like to work as a writer-editor while she took time out to have her baby. The job was for six months, and it got me going again. And my desk was in an open area surrounded by clerical staff, all women, each of whom thought I had stolen her job and ruined her chances for advancement. They begrudged my existence.

So I never asked for help. I asked for an IBM electric typewriter, and I did my own typing. Believe it or not, a lot of men at that time in our history did not know how to type and in fact thought it was effeminate to do so.

An aside: When I first started working on the Mount Hood National Forest in 1971, the Forest Supervisor caught me typing up a job classification and said, "We have women to do that." It caught me off guard, but I was pretty sharp that morning. I said, "I'm not typing. I'm composing." That was good enough for him, but I thought I caught the flicker of a smile on his face. And, of course, the reliance on computers later in my career put a keyboard on everyone's desk, senior male staff officers were no exception.

I had a great time at the Department of Education. My title was Writer-Editor. Single handedly, I published the monthly Education News, an eight-page, slick covered news bulletin for all the teachers in the state, complete with photos, and interviews of teachers and members of the Oregon Department of Education like George Katagiri, the father of outdoor education. I also put out the monthly Administrative Bulletin. And I put out a mimeographed monthly in-house news bulletin. I'll grumble a bit here a bit and say that the clerical pool would not help me collate and staple this one. Remember, I had the job they each thought belonged to them.

I also had the privilege of writing a speech for the Superintendent of Education, an elected position at that time. It was titled "One-Hundred Years of Education in Oregon." I had a lot of help on that one from a nice librarian at the State Library across the mall from our building. I would not have met my deadline without her.

My boss was named Evelyn, but I can't remember her last name. I wish I could. She once worked as the press secretary for the Governor of Colorado. She knew a lot about journalistic writing, and she was a pretty good teacher.

One fine sunny Friday, the Ways and Means committee members walked across the Capitol campus to our building, walked through our office, single file, and without saying a word walked back to the Capitol building. The next Monday our whole section received a pink slip giving us two weeks' notice. As a temp, I had no employment rights, so I just worked one week and said to hell with it and quit. Rumor had it that a presentation to that committee by a couple of people in our group was a sour mistake. I think that was the right guess.

Federal Service Entrance Examination

IN THOSE DAYS, ANYONE COULD show up at the Post Office on Saturday morning and take the FSEE (Federal Service Entrance Examination). My failed efforts to get on in a permanent job with the Fremont National Forest, my futile efforts to find myself a job, coupled with being pink slipped from the one my friend got me, left me without an income right in the middle of a huge recession in the country. So, I went to the Salem, Oregon post office on a Saturday morning and sat through several hours of written tests. I guess I scored pretty well because within a week or two I had offers of permanent employment from several agencies, but not the Forest Service.

Department of Defense

In need of an income, I took a job with the Department of Defense Contracting Office in Portland as a GS-7 trainee contracting officer. The pay looked pretty good after the trouble I'd had finding a job.

On one level, it was hilarious. The building had a stairway that ran four stories right up through the middle of the building, with doors on either side of each landing. I could look up and see the back wall of the fourth landing and stare at a big poster with a huge hand and a finger pointing at me. The poster read, "Remember, Security Begins and Ends with You."

And right in the middle of an open office area where I was assigned a desk was a big, gray safe…probably four feet square by three feet high. A heavy chain fastened with a padlock was wrapped around it, and a sign saying "Secret" hung from the chain. The boss was a man named Ed Pezolt. When he needed to open the safe, he'd say to the ten clerks working in the section to "Clear the room."

I had been drilled about the proper protocol for "secret" stuff. I had a "secret" clearance which in the Department of Defense didn't amount to much. I think even the janitors had a "secret" clearance. Anyway, if Ed wanted to open the safe, he had to clear the room, contact my "other" boss, a woman in charge of just about everything, who would open her safe and give Ed the key to the lock on the chain. I may misremember this, but I think she also kept the combination to the safe as well and would give it to Ed.

The first time Ed cleared the room, I got up to leave along with the clerks in our section. He said, "Not you."

I replied, "I don't want to know any secrets."

That got a laugh and he said, "Hell, there isn't anything in there you can't buy at the hardware store." And then he pulled open his top drawer, took out a key to the padlock, undid the chain, and started turning the dial. I left anyway.

I endured this insanity for five months. In five months, not one person asked me to have coffee, let alone lunch. I ate my brown bag lunch at my desk in an empty room.

It didn't take long to figure it out. It was just like my job at the Department of Education. The clerks all figured I had the job they should have gotten. I wonder how they would have treated the lucky person from the clerical pool had the job been offered to one of them.

Anyway, I was sick of putting together contracts for lumber purchases (remember, the Viet Nam War was in full swing at that time), which was a simple matter of checking boxes on a canned contract form. I mean that literally. Our office was basically just buying lots of lumber, so a long form was printed off and I was instructed as to which of the boilerplate clauses covered lumber purchases.

Along about this time, a friend from my OCE days, last name Aldrich (I can't remember his first name anymore) called and said he had a chance to teach at Linn-Benton Community College if he could find an English teacher to take his contract at Silverton High School. I jumped at the chance, interviewed with the principal at Silverton and was offered a job which I grabbed.

Other Events of the Year

I celebrated my 25th birthday on June 5, 1966. That day included a trip from Salem to Eugene to look at a Martin guitar a poor starving college student was selling for $75.00. He actually had two, and I bought them both for $150.00. I kept the spruce-faced Martin and sold the other to a friend for $75.00. (Those guitars are now worth about $3500 each.)

Alex Lafollette showed up at my party with a few of his friends and a pony keg. It turned out he was celebrating his birthday on June 5 as well. That was the start a close friendship which lasted over forty years.

Maggie and I decided to try and have a child.

Jennifer

On February 18, 1968, we became parents. Jennifer Margaret Collins was born in the Salem Memorial Hospital. It was a banner day for me. All I had hoped for was a healthy child, and Jennifer fit the bill.

The Collins family story of resilience, kindness. strength, and laughter

It was also a strange day. The nurses ran me out of the delivery room and out to the waiting area where some small couches and overstuffed chairs gave comfort to the anxious. It wasn't really a room, just a small space shared with an elevator. I guess you could call it an alcove for want of a better term.

The doors to the elevator opened, and a tall, older man with wavy silver hair stepped to an overstuffed chair, sat down, pulled a newspaper from under his arm and went to reading. He never said a word, but there was a whole lot of spooky going on because he looked exactly like Truman Collins, my grandfather. And my sense of it said he was keeping me company.

He stayed until the doctor came out to tell me I was the father of a healthy baby girl. Then, without a word, he folded up his newspaper, rose from his chair, stuffed the newspaper under his arm and walked to the elevator.

As he stepped into the elevator, and the doors slid shut, and I wondered what in the heck had just happened. I sometimes wonder if he would have spoken had the baby been a boy. He was a devout chauvinist.

I never really believed in ghosts, but I'm pretty sure Grandpa Truman was in the room, at least in spirit.

Silverton High School

OUR MOVE TO SILVERTON COULDN'T have come at a better time. Memory says Maggie's job with the Valley Migrant League was about to go away for lack of funds. But the school year was about to start.

We found a small two-bedroom house in Silverton, and I started a new adventure. At over one thousand students, Silverton High School was a whole lot bigger than North Marion. The sheer number of students made it a lot harder to get close to the students, and an experiment called Team Teaching led sometimes to a lecture hall style of teaching. I can say from first-hand experience, it doesn't work very well.

That aside, my team had the freshmen and sophomores, and the other team had the juniors and seniors. There were four of us on my team, and we were all brand new to the school.

In all there were eleven English Teachers, the eight people on the teams, two special ed teachers, and one chairman who did something along the lines of what we would expect of substitute teachers. If one of the ten of us was absent, he filled in. He was an older gentleman, and he was sick. He probably should not have still been working, but as an old guy myself these days, I can better understand the reluctance to "quit" anything. It's too permanent.

But to get on, this poor man would actually fall asleep in his classes, and it finally reached the point of the principal asking him to just finish the year as a back-up, no class prep that way, or as much pressure. And then I was appointed department Chairman. To this day, I still have no idea why.

I took it seriously. In looking at what we were about, I decided the only teachers providing anything practical for students were the shop teachers (mechanics, welding, and woodworking), the home economics teacher, and the agriculture teacher. Basically, we were pumping almost one hundred percent of our students through a college preparatory program from which only about ten percent would actually go on to college, and from that group maybe half would actually matriculate from college. Five percent success is a miserable number.

Angel Job Corps Center

I KEPT HEARING GOOD THINGS about the Forest Service Job Corps program, so I called the Siuslaw National Forest and wound up talking to the Center Director of the Angel Job Corps Center near Waldport on the Oregon Coast. I asked if I could send one of "my" teachers to work the summer and find out how the Job Corps was succeeding with our failures. He said they would hire one of us as a GS-9 temporary for the summer.

When I offered this to the English teachers, they all turned me down. So...I took the job myself. Summer came and we moved into an apartment in Waldport, about ten minutes from Angel Job Corps Center, an all-boys center.

To keep a long story short, Job Corps was taking kids off the street, some from Watts in Los Angeles, some from Cleveland, Ohio, some from Alaska, and a mix of Oregon kids, a lot of whom had rap sheets. The program gave them basic reading and math skills, and then moved them into programs teaching them practical skills like painting, carpentry, cooking, concrete work, sheet rock...basic blue-collar work. And the teachers were card carrying Union members. When a student finished the course work which generally took a full year, he was sponsored and hired as an apprentice by the union. And looked after by the union members. The whole process was called The World of Work Program.

The Collins family story of resilience, kindness. strength, and laughter

I was impressed. When I returned to Silverton at the end of summer, I was determined to adopt the World of Work Program for Silverton High School. I sketched my idea of how we could run one in conjunction with the regular school program and sold the idea to the principal and to the district superintendent. I was told to recruit someone with a blue-collar background to run the program.

I found a man who also had a teaching degree, a fellow who had at various times been a strike breaker, a union organizer, a farmer, a mechanic, a race car builder, and a race car driver. I offered him the job and he jumped at the chance. But when it came time to give him a contract, the district superintendent objected. Apparently, the superintendent had taken a graduate level program with my hire and didn't like my guy at all.

I pressed my case but failed to budge the superintendent. I dropped the whole idea. I wrote a letter to Emmett High School in Idaho, and one to Weiser High School in Idaho. I had two job offers on the same day and took the Weiser job.

And that's how we wound up in Idaho for nearly two years.

Catherine

CATHERINE WAS BORN ON APRIL 9, 1969 while we were still living in Silverton. It was once again off to Salem Memorial Hospital. And again, I sat in the waiting area, but no old men came to sit with me. Nonetheless, it was another glorious event, and I wept again in relief and joy to have another baby daughter. It was another red-letter day for me.

I'll just say one thing before I close this part: I have long believed no child should be an "only" child. I think it cheats them out of the joy of brothers and sisters, our traveling companions on this trip through life.

I hope this wandering tale answers some of the questions my children and grandchildren might find when they, too, approach the edge of old age.

Rod

www.ingramcontent.com/pod-product-compliance
Lightning Source LLC
Chambersburg PA
CBHW020427010526
44118CB00010B/458